A GEOGRAPHY OF
GHANA

TO MY PARENTS

A GEOGRAPHY OF GHANA

BY

E. A. BOATENG

B. LITT., M.A. (OXON.)

*Professor of Geography at the University
of Ghana*

SECOND EDITION

CAMBRIDGE
AT THE UNIVERSITY PRESS
1966

PUBLISHED BY
THE SYNDICS OF THE CAMBRIDGE UNIVERSITY PRESS
Bentley House, 200 Euston Road, London, N.W. 1
American Branch: 32 East 57th Street, New York, N.Y. 10022
West African Office: P.M.B. 5181, Ibadan, Nigeria

©

CAMBRIDGE UNIVERSITY PRESS
1966

First edition 1959
Reprinted 1960
Second edition 1966

Printed in Great Britain at the University Printing House, Cambridge
(Brooke Crutchley, University Printer)

LIBRARY OF CONGRESS CATALOGUE
CARD NUMBER: 65-22922

PREFACE

This book is intended primarily for students preparing for the School Certificate Examination and the G.C.E. in West Africa, for whom at present no suitable textbook on the geography of Ghana exists. It is hoped, however, that first-year University students and others with more general interests will find it useful as an introductory study.

I have assumed that the majority of my readers will already be familiar with the basic terminology and principles of elementary physical geography and map-work, and therefore, although I have tried to make the presentation as simple as possible, I have made little attempt to explain the few technical terms whose use was felt to be necessary now and again in the interests of clearness and brevity.

Even so, many of the names of geological formations in Ghana, which appear in chapter 2 and, to a less extent, in chapter 12, are likely to be unfamiliar. Most of these names were first coined by the Ghana Geological Survey, and their use has tended to be confined to their own highly technical publications. While fully conscious of the difficulties likely to be presented by such unfamiliar and often lengthy terms, I consider that they form part of the essential 'grammar' of the subject, and at the level for which this book is intended there is nothing to be gained by postponing acquaintance with them. A good, up-to-date geological map will enable the student to understand these terms and also to grasp the outlines of Ghana's geology, which should provide a useful foundation for more advanced work later.

Other terms likely to be unfamiliar are the names of the regions into which the country has been divided for purposes of geographical study and those of a few natural features such as mountain ranges and conspicuous lowland areas. Many of these are names which I have had to devise myself, and although space

v

has not enabled me to argue the case for their choice fully, the reasons behind them can be deduced easily in most cases. The geography of Ghana stands in great need of such nomenclature, and I hope that some of the terms I have used, if not all, will commend themselves for adoption into current usage.

The book is divided into three parts. Parts I and II deal with the physical and human geography of the whole country treated under a number of general headings, while in part III the country is divided into its component geographical regions and the salient features of each region are discussed in turn. It is hoped in this way to enable the reader to visualize the actual face of the land and to see the variations which have come about as a result of local differences in physical conditions and human activity. Several maps and diagrams have been provided as an aid to clearer understanding, but the student is advised to supplement these as much as possible with large-scale topographical maps of Ghana, such as the 1:62,500, 1:125,000 and 1:250,000 series prepared by the Survey Department.

Although this book is based largely on the results of my own field-work, I have obtained a great deal of information from a wide range of publications, including many official documents and maps. These sources are acknowledged in the text, but I must thank the Government Archivist, Accra, the Ghana High Commissioner's Office and the library of the Commonwealth Relations Office in London for giving me access to many of them.

I must also express my gratitude to the large number of people who have assisted me with information and in other ways, but I wish to thank specially Professor L. J. Lewis of the Institute of Education, University College of Ghana, for his help and encouragement in the early stages of the work, and my former tutor and research supervisor, Professor R. W. Steel, for sparing the time to read through my manuscript and to offer several helpful comments and suggestions.

I feel particularly indebted to Professor H. C. Darby and other members of the department of geography at University College London for their kindness and help during the spring and summer

of 1957, when I held an Honorary Research Assistantship in the
department and College. One of the many benefits of this association is that besides giving me a convenient base in London for
the completion of my manuscript, it has enabled me to obtain the
services of the department's cartographic section, whose skilled
staff have drawn practically all the maps and diagrams. The rest
of the maps and diagrams have been drawn by the technical staff
of the geography department of the University College of Ghana,
for whose services I am equally grateful.

The writing of this book, particularly during the final stages
when I have been away from Ghana and, therefore, able somehow
to see it in clearer perspective, has been for me a most stimulating
and pleasant experience, and I offer what I have been able to put
together as a modest contribution to the fuller understanding of
the geographical character and possibilities of our young country,
without which it will be impossible to make a sober assessment of
our position in the modern world.

E. A. BOATENG

Department of Geography
University College London
August 1957

PREFACE TO THE SECOND EDITION

Since this book was first written eight years ago very many changes have taken place over the face of Ghana. In some cases whole landscapes have been transformed out of all recognition in consequence of bold development plans launched since the country attained its independence. In 1960 the country successfully conducted a modern population census far ahead of any previous census in thoroughness and accuracy. As I write, the vast new Lake Volta is steadily forming behind the dam at Akosombo which was completed only two days ago, and work on the aluminium smelter at Tema is proceeding apace.

It was inevitable that in the face of all these changes a great deal of what was written in 1957 or even at the subsequent reprinting of the book in 1960 should now be obsolete. No geography book can ever hope to be wholly up to date, at least in respect of economic and human facts. Nevertheless, advantage has been taken of this new edition to bring essential material as up to date as possible and also to correct errors in the earlier edition which I have detected or which have been brought to my attention by the kindness of friends. I wish in particular to thank Professor W. J. McCallien for his helpful criticisms and suggestions in connection with the chapter 'Relief and Structure', which, though embodied in the 1960 reprint, it was not possible then to acknowledge. I wish also to thank the cartographic staff of my department who have redrawn many of the maps and diagrams. Finally, I must acknowledge the debt I owe to my readers, including many in Ghana, for the warm response accorded to this book since its first appearance in 1959.

E. A. BOATENG

Department of Geography
University of Ghana
Legon

10 February 1965

CONTENTS

LIST OF ILLUSTRATIONS

TEXT FIGURES

LIST OF ILLUSTRATIONS

LIST OF ILLUSTRATIONS

LIST OF ILLUSTRATIONS

LIST OF ILLUSTRATIONS

ACKNOWLEDGEMENTS

The following photographs are reproduced by permission of Ghana Information Service:

Plates 1, 2*a*, 4, 5, 6*b*, 8, 9*a*, 9*b*, 10, 11*a*, 11*b*, 12*a*, 12*b*, 13, 14*a*, 14*b*, 15*a*, 16*a*, 16*b*, 17*b*, 19*b*, 20*a*, 22*b*, 23*a*, 23*b*, 24.

Plates 17*a*, 18*b* and 21*b* are Crown Copyright.

Plate 20*b* is reproduced by courtesy of the Volta River Authority, Accra.

All the other photographs were taken by the author or under his direction.

LIST OF TABLES

PART I

THE LAND

1

GHANA TODAY

I. POSITION AND EXTENT

Ghana is almost centrally placed among the countries strung along the Guinea coast. East of it lies Togoland, beyond which are Dahomey and the large Federation of Nigeria. To the west are Ivory Coast, Liberia, Sierra Leone, Guinea, Portuguese Guinea, and Senegal, which is almost divided into two by the Gambia.

All these countries reach down to the coast, but on their inland boundaries are other countries belonging to the vast region formerly known collectively as French West Africa or *Afrique Occidentale Française*. One of these inland countries, Upper Volta, lies along the northern boundary of Ghana (Fig. 1).

The southern coast of Ghana extends between latitude $4\frac{1}{2}°$ North at Cape Three Points and $6\frac{1}{2}°$ North in the extreme east, and is thus not far from the equator. From the coast the country extends inland to about latitude $11°$ North, thus covering a distance of some 420 miles from south to north. The distance across the widest part from east to west is rather less, measuring about 334 miles between longitude $1\frac{1}{2}°$ East and longitude $3\frac{1}{2}°$ West. The Meridian of Greenwich, which passes through eastern England, also runs through the eastern half of Ghana, cutting the coast exactly at the new port of Tema, where there was once a rock jutting out in the sea known as the Meridian Rock.

In 1957 Ghana was the only independent West African country in the British Commonwealth. Since then, however, the remaining British colonies, Nigeria, Sierra Leone and the Gambia, in that order, have all achieved independence. The total area of the country is 92,100 square miles, and the population, according to the last census in 1960, is 6,726,815, distributed as shown in Table 1.

Although the other Commonwealth countries in West Africa are

3

not very far away, the fact that Ghana is surrounded on all sides, except along the south, by countries formerly ruled by France has prevented it from having direct contacts with any of these countries except by sea. This has presented a number of difficulties, which have only recently been overcome in part by the increased use of air transport.

	Area (in square miles)	Population
Eastern Region	8,693	1,586,013
Central Region	3,815	751,392
Western Region	9,236	626,155
Ashanti Region	9,417	1,109,133
Brong-Ahafo Region	15,273	587,920
Northern Region	27,175	531,573
Upper Region	10,548	757,344
Volta Region	7,943	777,285
Total	92,100	6,726,815

Table 1. *Population distribution in 1960*

Like other parts of the Guinea coast, Ghana's southern stretch of coast is marked by strong surf, which pounds incessantly against a shore that is entirely without any natural harbours in which ships can anchor safely. Consequently, except at Takoradi and Tema (completed in 1961) where artificial harbours have been constructed at great expense, ocean-going ships had to anchor about half a mile out to sea in open *roadsteads*. Only comparatively small surf-boats could make the perilous journey between the shore and the deeper and calmer water beyond the thundering surf. Today all the roadstead ports have been closed and all the country's overseas trade passes through Takoradi and Tema. Hardly any off-shore islands break the monotony of the coast, and apart from a few volcanic islands studding the Southern Atlantic, nothing except a waste of water lies between our shores and the continent of Antarctica 5200 miles away.

2. POLITICAL GROWTH

Before the country attained its independence on 6 March 1957 and assumed the new name of *Ghana*, it was known as the 'Gold Coast'. Despite its familiarity, the term 'Gold Coast' is of foreign origin

4

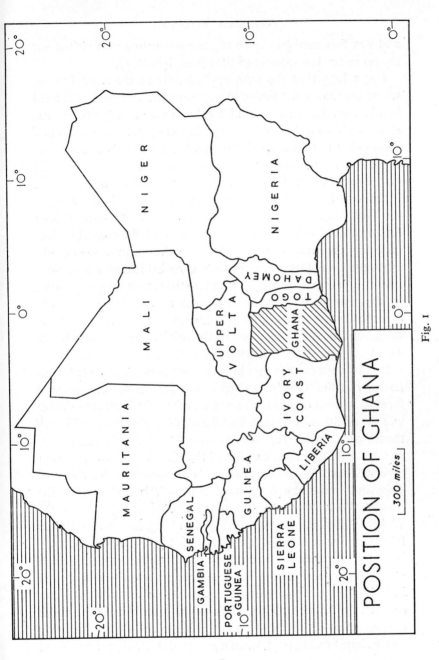

POSITION OF GHANA

300 miles

Fig. 1

5

and was first used by the Portuguese navigators who visited our shores in the last quarter of the fifteenth century.

For a long time the term applied only to the coastal areas, where the Europeans traded in gold supplied to them by the local inhabitants. The term 'Gold Coast' was very apt, for before the slave trade overshadowed everything else, gold was the chief commodity obtained by Europeans from these shores. Beyond the coastal region lay the kingdom of Ashanti, which was bordered on the north by territory that was almost unknown to Europeans.

Not one, but several, European powers engaged in the trade of the 'Gold Coast', but by the end of the nineteenth century Britain had ousted all of them and alone controlled the coastal region, including the many forts built by such European powers as the Portuguese, the Danes and the Dutch. As British influence spread inland, first into Ashanti and then into the region formerly known as the 'Northern Territories', so the term 'Gold Coast' was extended to the whole of this British *sphere of influence*, while at the same time a small section of the original coastal strip in the west went over to the French as part of the Ivory Coast.

Roughly, we can say that by 1906 the boundaries of the British territory of the 'Gold Coast' had been determined in their final form by various *Orders in Council*, and the only significant change was the addition of 'British Togoland', following the partition of the former German Togoland between Great Britain and France as a result of Germany's defeat in the First World War. In 1921 'British Togoland' was known as 'The Mandated Territory of Togoland under the League of Nations', but at end of the Second World War when Germany was again defeated by the Western Allies its name was changed to 'Togoland under United Kingdom Trusteeship'. Today it is an integral part of Ghana.

It must be emphasized that throughout this process of partition and boundary-making the European powers concerned consulted their own interests primarily, rather than the wishes of the African peoples. In isolated places chiefs would place themselves under the protection of the European power in control of a neighbouring fort, as happened in 1844, when a group of chiefs signed the 'Bond

6

of 1844' with Britain, but usually the people had little say in the drawing of international boundaries through their lands. The result was that these boundaries frequently cut across whole tribes and their land and also brought together within the same political framework people who in most cases had never formed a single united political entity.

In what was formerly known as 'the Colony', for example, were to be found a large number of states which were autonomous and quite independent of one another. They might have dealings with their neighbours from time to time, but there was no question of belonging to the same state in the modern sense of the term, and it was the same with the people of the former 'Northern Territories'.

Only in Ashanti was there a significant degree of unity. Here, a line of powerful kings from Osei Tutu onwards had gradually welded a large number of states together into a single political unit known as the Ashanti Confederacy, which was busily engaged in conquering nearby states and expanding its territory.

In 1946, there were something like 108 Native States in Ghana, ranging in size from 25 to 2000 square miles, and in population from 2000 to 228,000 people. Each state has its own paramount or head chief with, under him, a number of divisional or subordinate chiefs.

Until the beginning of the present century wars were common in the country, as in most parts of West Africa, and one of the most effective ways of ensuring protection against attack was membership of a powerful state. Sometimes, places lying far distant from a powerful chief would attach themselves to his state as a protection against their immediate neighbours. This served to produce a somewhat complicated pattern of states, and it is largely responsible for the many 'islands' which some states still possess within the territory of other neighbouring states (Fig. 2).

Along the coast the presence of forts owned by rival European powers produced further fragmentation among some of the nearby states. Hence, today, we have such 'fort kingdoms' as British Sekondi, Dutch Sekondi, James Town and Ussher Town.

Few states had properly defined boundaries; instead, they were

7

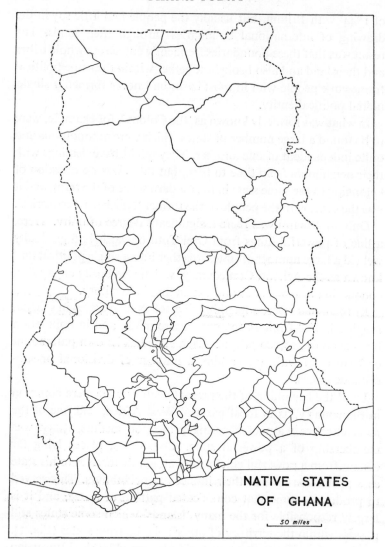

Fig. 2. Native States of Ghana (based on Survey Department map of 1946).

separated from each other by vague frontier zones that oscillated from time to time with the changing fortunes of war. Even today many of our inter-state boundaries are still in dispute.

The system of indirect rule introduced by the British government employed the chiefs as agents of local government and thus helped to perpetuate the office and the pattern of Native States in the country. Groups of states were formed into larger administrative units known as *districts*, and these in turn were grouped into *provinces* within the larger divisions of the 'Colony', 'Ashanti', 'Northern Territories' and 'Togoland'.

The result of all this has been to bring the Native States closer together gradually within common administrative divisions governed from Accra, the capital. Therefore, although the Native States remain, a great deal of their former independence has disappeared. That, however, does not alter the fact that as a political unit, Ghana, as we know it today, began largely as an artificial creation imposed by European powers, and not something that grew naturally and spontaneously through the efforts and wishes of the people themselves.

Today, for purposes of government, the country is divided into eight regions: the Eastern, Central and Western Regions, corresponding to the eastern and western parts of the former Gold Coast Colony; the Ashanti and Brong-Ahafo Regions, formerly known as Ashanti; the Northern and Upper Regions, corresponding to the southern and northern parts of the former Northern Territories and the northern part of Togoland; and the Volta Region, which mainly represents the southern part of Togoland. Each of these regions is further subdivided into administrative districts (Fig. 3). Government is centralized in the National Assembly at Accra, but each region has a regional Commissioner, under whom are a number of district commissioners. The Native States are still recognized, but the chiefs are primarily concerned with traditional and customary matters in the country.

Now that independence has been achieved, Ghana is faced with the crucial task of turning its artificial association of diverse elements into a single, united state commanding the loyalty of all its citizens. This is no easy task, for whereas many nations in the world today have had centuries in which to accomplish it, we

9

must endeavour to achieve it almost immediately in order to hold our own in the difficult conditions of the present-day world.

In addition, there still remains the equally important question of settling any existing boundary disputes with the former French territories next door to us, whose political development has been along entirely different lines. With them, as with the other independent states of Africa, our guiding rule for the future must obviously be CO-OPERATION.

Much has been done in this direction already. The Second World War brought the governments of all the British West African territories closely together, and since Ghana obtained her independence in 1957, the first President, Dr Kwame Nkrumah, has made vigorous efforts to secure a Union Government for the entire continent of Africa.

Although several of the services formerly run jointly by the British territories have been abolished, there is still a wide range of technical and scientific matters, such as the eradication of tsetse and the control of locusts and other pests, which have formed and will continue to form the subject of frequent consultations among the different governments.

ADMINISTRATIVE DIVISIONS

NOTE. *Several changes have taken place in the administrative divisions of Ghana since independence. Fig. 3 shows the position at the beginning of 1965.*

Fig. 3

2

RELIEF AND STRUCTURE

Like the rest of West Africa and indeed the whole of Africa south of the Atlas Mountains, Ghana forms part of the ancient continent of *Gondwanaland* which is supposed to have split up into separate continents at the beginning of the *Mesozoic Era* (Fig. 4*a* and *b*). With the exception of the immediate coastal fringes, which have been covered at intervals by the sea, and a few inland areas, most of the land has stood above sea-level for some 200,000,000 years. During this period it has been subjected to prolonged sub-aerial erosion.

Some of the rocks bear traces of intense folding, but it is fairly certain that this occurred in *Pre-Cambrian* and *Palaeozoic* times, and most of the mountain chains which the folding produced have long since been worn down. Owing to the hardness of the rocks, however, the roots of some of these ancient mountains are still preserved in the form of hills and ridges standing above neighbouring areas of softer and more easily eroded rocks. Mountains produced by this kind of differential erosion are very widespread in Ghana.

Their usual direction is from north-east to south-west, in accordance with the original folding. This trend is prevalent not only in Ghana but in many parts of West Africa and shows that the earth movements responsible for it took place over a wide area (Figs. 5 and 6).

Some of the ancient earth movements were accompanied by volcanic activity and faulting. In the Tarkwa region, for example, laccoliths, sills and dykes of varying sizes are found together with a number of faults in the rocks, but it is in the eastern part, north of Kpandu, that the most extensive masses of volcanic rock in Ghana occur.

In addition to these localized features, changes in sea-level

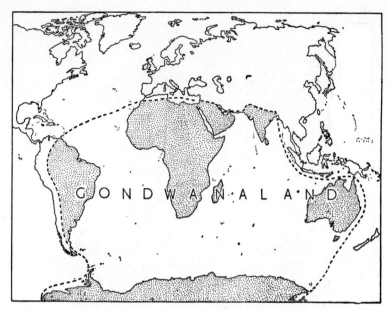

Fig. 4a. Gondwanaland (after Holmes and Read).

GEOLOGICAL TIME SCALE

ERAS	PERIODS AND SYSTEMS	REPRESENTATIVE ROCK TYPES IN GHANA	AGE (in millions of years)
KAINOZOIC	Quaternary	Superficial deposits or Mantle rock	
			1
	Tertiary	Deposits in Volta delta and coastal Nzima regions and also probably sediments found at Saltpond	70
	Cretaceous		
MESOZOIC (Secondary)	Jurassic		120
	Triassic		150
			190
	Permian		
	Carboniferous	Uncertain	220
PALAEOZOIC (Primary)	Devonian	Accraian and Sekondian	280
	Silurian		320
	Ordovician	Undifferentiated representatives possibly in Voltaian	350
	Cambrian		400
			500

PRE-CAMBRIAN ERAS   at least 1,750

Represented in Ghana by: Dahomeyan, Birrimian, Tarkwaian, Togo series (Akwapimian), Buem.

Fig. 4b

13

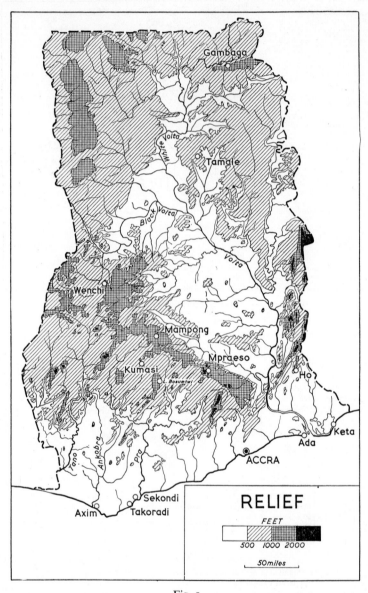

Fig. 5

14

TREND LINES OF PAST FOLDING

After Junner

50 miles

Fig. 6

15

caused by climatic fluctuations during the *Quaternary* Ice Age have produced a series of distinct erosion surfaces or peneplains throughout the country.[1] At certain points near the sea, such as Sekondi, it is possible to see some of the former sea cliffs and beaches standing high above the present level of the sea and providing good examples of raised beaches.

GEOLOGY

The geological map (Fig. 7) shows that there is a wide extent of rocks in the centre of Ghana known as *Voltaian*. These rocks, which are so named because they occur in the basin of the river Volta, consist mainly of thick series of sandstone, with shales, conglomerates and a few limestones. Covering something like 45 per cent of the total surface area of the country, the Voltaian rocks are more extensive than any other single system of rocks.

The Voltaian beds occur as almost horizontal or only slightly folded strata and give rise to flat-topped or tabular relief of moderate height averaging 500 ft. above sea-level, except along the southern and northern edges, where they form high plateaus standing about 1750 ft. above sea-level, marked by impressive outward-facing scarps. On the inner sides of these plateaus, also, scarps are found, but they are generally lower and much less striking. A convenient name for the plateau on the south is the SOUTHERN VOLTAIAN PLATEAU or KWAHU PLATEAU, whilst the northern one may be called the GAMBAGA PLATEAU. The basin of the Volta itself forms the VOLTAIAN BASIN.

East of the Voltaian Basin is a narrow mountainous zone with a north-east to south-west trend extending from the eastern boundary of the country to within a few miles of the sea west of Accra. The component rocks are known as the *Buem* and *Togo* series. They are older than the Voltaian, being of late Pre-Cambrian age, but have many points of resemblance with them.

The Buem series, which is younger than the Togo series, consists largely of shales of various kinds, sandstones and basalt

[1] N. R. Junner, 'Progress in Geological and Mineral Investigations in the Gold Coast'. *Gold Coast Geological Survey Bulletin No. 16* (1946).

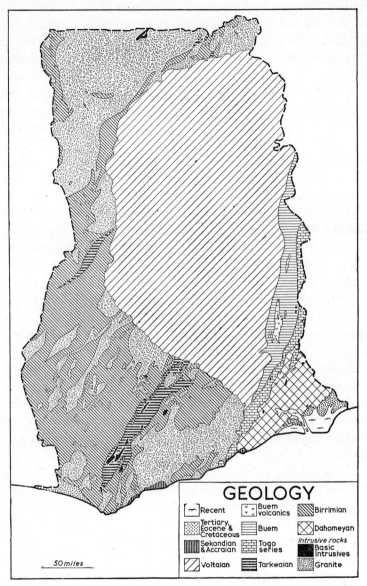

GEOLOGY

⌇ Recent	˅˅ Buem volcanics	⧄ Birrimian
Tertiary, Eocene & Cretaceous	☰ Buem	⧅ Dahomeyan
Sekondian & Accraian	Togo series	*Intrusive rocks* Basic Intrusives
⧄ Voltaian	▬ Tarkwaian	Granite

50 miles

Fig. 7

derived from ancient volcanoes. The Togo series also contains sandstones and shales usually metamorphosed to quartzite and phyllite, which has led some geologists to suppose that it represents a metamorphosed version of the Buem and Voltaian series.

Both the Buem and Togo series, particularly the latter, are highly folded, and form the striking ranges of hills known as the AKWAPIM-TOGO RANGES, which coincide with them and extend from the mouth of the Densu in a north-easterly direction right up to the Togoland frontier, beyond which they continue through French territory to the river Niger as the TOGO-ATAKORA MOUNTAINS.

As a whole, this range is one of the most striking features in the relief of West Africa. It consists not just of a single fold, but of a complex of folds sometimes very closely packed together. In Ghana its average height is 1500 ft. above sea-level, but isolated peaks, especially in Togoland, attain altitudes of up to nearly 3000 ft. Although the general direction of the range is from north-east to the south-west, north of Kpandu there is a branch with an almost north-south trend. This section comprises folds developed in the Buem series, and some of the higher parts are associated with masses of basalt.

Despite the fact that erosion has acted on the folds for a long period, the range still has the internal characteristics of a folded mountain, and in roadside cuttings and other places where the rocks are exposed it is possible to see clear signs of folding in them.

The small triangular area between the Akwapim-Togo Ranges and the sea is of considerable geological interest because it contains at once some of the oldest and youngest rocks in the country. First, there is a broad band of Pre-Cambrian, possibly *Archaean*, rocks, which are described in Ghana as *Dahomeyan*. The Dahomeyan rocks lie immediately to the east of the Akwapim-Togo Ranges and consist largely of various types of schists and gneisses containing a deep red, transparent mineral known as garnet. Generally, they give rise to a low and undulating relief, but in the Shai country between Dodowa and Akuse is a series of steep-sided hills composed of gneiss rising abruptly from the surrounding plains. These hills, some of which rise to 1400 ft. above sea-level, have been described as *inselbergs*.[1]

Practically the whole of the triangle east of the Akwapim-Togo Ranges forms the ACCRA COASTAL AND INTERIOR PLAINS, but in the extreme south-eastern corner, between the Dahomeyan rocks and the sea, is a distinct physical division, the VOLTA DELTA, which is composed of young deposits ranging in age from Upper Cretaceous to Recent. The land here is flat and almost featureless and several large lagoons are found between the sea and the Volta. The Recent deposits have been brought down by the Volta and other streams and built into a vast delta, whose arcuate edge now extends further out into the sea than the original coastline.

To the south, west and north of the Voltaian Basin is a large area composed predominantly of Pre-Cambrian rocks and in-truded granites. Two main series are recognized, the *Birrimian* and the *Tarkwaian*. The Birrimian series is the older and more ex-tensive of the two. It consists of metamorphosed lavas, various intrusive rocks, phyllites, schists and volcanic ash, known as tuffs. The Tarkwaian series, which occurs in narrow zones with a characteristic north-east to south-west trend in the Birrimian, consists of quartzites, phyllites, schists and conglomerates. Both the Birrimian and the Tarkwaian bear traces of intense folding in the past, but all the mountains to which this folding gave rise have been worn down long ago, leaving only a few roots and resistant beds as upstanding masses today.

No extensive areas of high land are associated with either the Birrimian or the Tarkwaian series, and the areas where they occur have an average elevation of up to 1000 ft., with only a few isolated ridges reaching 1500 or 2000 ft. These ridges are in-variably the result of the differential erosion of beds of varying hardness.

On the basis of landforms the vast area of Pre-Cambrian rocks

[1] N. R. Junner, 'Geology of the Gold Coast and Western Togoland', *Gold Coast Geological Survey Bulletin No. 11* (1940).

2-2

and intruded granites containing the Birrimian and Tarkwaian series can be divided broadly into a south-western section and a north-western one. The former, which lies largely in Akan country, may be called the AKAN DISSECTED PENEPLAIN, while the north-western section may be called the WA-NAVRONGO-BAWKU DISSECTED PENEPLAIN. In both areas prolonged erosion has produced a generally uniform surface or series of surfaces on which present-day rivers are busy carving out their valleys.

From an economic point of view the Tarkwaian and Birrimian rocks are extremely important. Most of the gold, diamonds, and manganese obtained in Ghana is derived from Birrimian rocks, whilst the Tarkwaian also yield considerable quantities of gold. In addition rich deposits of bauxite occur in the areas covered by these two types of rocks, although bauxite is also found on the Southern Voltaian Plateau, as at Ejuanema (see p. 170).

The Tarkwaian and Birrimian rocks are actually more extensive than they appear to be, for we assume that they extend underneath the Voltaian beds at great depth.

The granitic intrusions which are so extensive in the dissected peneplains of Pre-Cambrian rocks are usually divided into an older section called *Cape Coast Granite* and a younger section called *Dixcove Granite*. Cape Coast Granite is more predominant in the Wa-Navrongo-Bawku area. Generally speaking, granite gives rise to relief characterized by a large number of small, rounded hills surmounted by *tors* and separated by narrow valleys. This kind of relief is well shown between Nsawam and Cape Coast, where it has a marked effect on the roads, causing them to turn and twist almost dangerously.

The Tarkwaian, Birrimian and the associated granites reach the sea between Senya Beraku and the western boundary of Ghana. At various points along the coast, however, small areas of younger rocks occur, many of them too small to appear on a geological map drawn on the scale of Fig. 7. Between Elmina and Takoradi, for example, are found certain sandstones, shales, conglomerates and limestones of Upper-Palaeozoic age, which are known as the *Sekondian*. They belong to the same age as some sandstones, grits and shales at Accra, known as the *Accraian*. At Saltpond is a small area of Tertiary beds, while between Esiama and Half Assini are more deposits of Tertiary rocks composed of shales, sandstones and limestones of marine origin. There are also some sands in these beds which are of considerable economic interest because they are thought to contain oil.

Finally, something must be said about the coastal features. All along the coast of Ghana the waves are continuously pounding against the shore. The character of each particular stretch of coast depends on the nature of the local rock structure and on the relief. Hard rocks, or those that are protected against rapid destruction, tend to stick out as promontories or headlands, whose dismembered ends may form *stacks*, such as those between the Bishop's Boys' School and the harbour at Accra or at Sekondi.

Where the rocks are more easily eroded bays may form in which sand often accumulates readily. The stretch of coast between Cape Three Points and Accra consists of a succession of bays and headlands, and lagoons are comparatively rare. To the east and west of this area the land is much flatter near the sea, and lagoons tend to be formed where the mouths of rivers are ponded back by the action of the surf and currents of the sea. At the mouth of the Volta the lagoons are particularly large and form part of the delta. The coast of Ghana can therefore be divided broadly into three: west of Cape Three Points is the *lagoon coast*, between Cape Three Points and Accra is the *promontory coast*, while east of Accra, at the mouth of the Volta, is the *delta coast*.

3

CLIMATE AND WEATHER

The climate of a place is determined by the average weather conditions found there. Weather itself is the result of the activity and conditions of the atmosphere. The earth is surrounded by a film of air some 200 miles thick, and all the radiation reaching it from the sun must pass through this film. A certain proportion of the sun's radiation affects the atmosphere directly in its passage to the earth, but quite a lot of the atmosphere's heat is derived from what is reflected back into it after reaching the earth.

Human beings, plants and animals live on the earth's surface and it is therefore the lower layers of the atmosphere that really affect them. But indirectly everything that happens throughout the atmosphere has some effect on life on the earth.

The climate of any particular place can be broken down into a number of *elements* or component parts. These elements are those features which can be measured or observed, such as temperature, the humidity of the air, rainfall, the direction and speed of the wind, the amount of sunshine, the amount and nature of the clouds and several other less significant things.

Each of these elements is caused by the working of a number of *factors* or determining causes. Thus, the latitude of a place, its altitude or height above sea-level, its distance from the sea, its position in relation to land masses and the sea are all important factors of climate. It is not always easy to draw a hard and fast line between elements and factors, for there are some elements which are responsible for still other elements, and are therefore elements in one sense and factors in another. A good example is wind direction, which can have considerable influence on temperature and rainfall, although in itself it is an important element of climate.

The connection between weather and climate needs to be made a little clearer. Anyone who looks at the sky knows that its appearance is continually changing. Sometimes the change may be so slow as not to be readily apparent, but at other times the rate of change is quite striking. The state of the atmosphere at any particular point of time at any place is really the weather; in order to have an idea of the atmospheric conditions which are generally found there it is necessary to consider the weather conditions over a very much longer period. *Thirty* or *thirty-five years* is considered a convenient period for this purpose by meteorologists, who are concerned with the detailed study of the various processes taking place in the atmosphere.

Useful though a knowledge of average conditions is, it is not by itself enough. From a practical point of view it is essential to know the different types of weather which tend to occur in any area as well as some of the peculiar types which occur only occasionally. A farmer, for example, who knows that the average rainfall in the area where he grows his crops is 50 in. a year, is in a much better position to make provision for the future if he also knows that it is possible for the rainfall to drop to 20 in. or rise to 65 in. during certain years. In the one case he may have a reserve supply of water handy to be used on his farm if the need should arise, and in the other case he may lay out his farm in such a way that an unusually heavy rainfall does not flood his land, destroy the crops or carry the good soil away.

Farmers are so dependent on the weather and climate that they often have a much more intimate knowledge of their nature based on practical experience over a long period of personal observation than people who rely solely on what books and figures dealing with average conditions tell them.

Climatic phenomena are not influenced in any way by political boundaries. Winds, for example, which are responsible for carrying moisture and temperature conditions from one place to another, circle freely round the whole earth. To understand the climate of a single country like Ghana it is therefore necessary to know the broad outlines of climate over a much wider area, if not the whole earth.

In the part of Africa where Ghana lies there are two main

systems of winds (Figs. 8 and 9). Blowing from the Sahara desert, where temperatures are very high, come the north-east trades or Harmattan, as they are called locally. These winds are hot and dry. Opposed to them from the sea blow the south-west winds, which are really the south-east trades that have been deflected on crossing the equator. The south-west winds are cool and moist because of their passage across the sea.

In popular speech these two sets of moving air are referred to as winds, but meteorologists prefer to think of them as large bodies of air or *air masses*, whose movements are conveyed to us in the form of winds. Whether they are referred to as winds or air masses, it must be remembered that it is not just a thin film of air that is moving, but large masses of air several thousand feet thick, each with its distinctive characteristics. Because of its origin from the continental interior, the northern air mass is described as the *Tropical Continental Air Mass*, while the southern one from across the sea is described as the *Tropical Maritime (or Equatorial) Air Mass*. The zone where the two meet is known as the *Inter-Tropical Convergence Zone*.[1]

The names given to the air masses in West Africa sound rather long and difficult, and for the sake of convenience we can substitute much simpler terms and speak of the north-east trades, blowing from the Sahara desert towards the Guinea coast, and the monsoon or south-west winds, blowing from the South Atlantic towards the Guinea coast. Most of the weather and climatic conditions experienced in West Africa are the result of one of these two sets of winds or of their joint effect.

The Tropical Maritime or Equatorial Air Mass comes mostly from the South Atlantic and therefore has a long history of travel across the sea before reaching the Guinea coast as the south-west monsoon. The surface layers of this air mass are generally cool and moist and temperatures in it decrease fairly slowly with height. The relative humidity (see p. 35) remains constant up to a height of about 6000 ft., but falls off rapidly after this.

[1] See F. K. Hare, *The Restless Atmosphere*, Hutchinson's University Library (London, 1953)

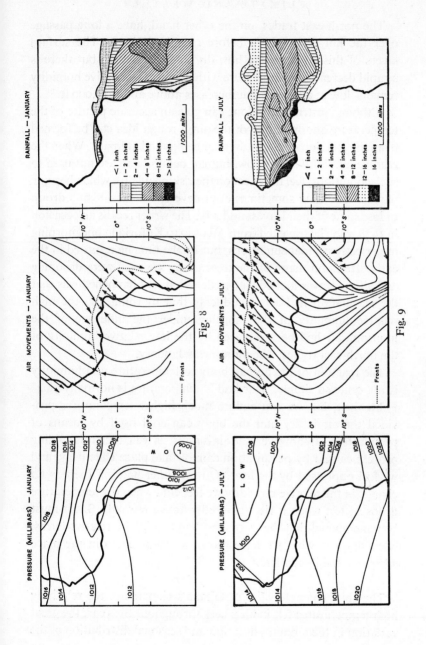

PRESSURE (MILLIBARS) — JANUARY

AIR MOVEMENTS — JANUARY

RAINFALL — JANUARY

< 1 inch
1 — 2 inches
2 — 4 inches
4 — 8 inches
8 —12 inches
> 12 inches

Fronts ....

1000 miles

Fig. 8

PRESSURE (MILLIBARS) — JULY

AIR MOVEMENTS — JULY

RAINFALL — JULY

< 1 inch
1 — 2 inches
2 — 4 inches
4 — 8 inches
8 —12 inches
12 —16 inches
16 inches

Fronts ....

1000 miles

Fig. 9

25

The north-east trades, on the other hand, have a long passage over the hot, dry Sahara before reaching Ghana. The surface layers of this air mass are hot, dry and dust-laden, but there is a rapid decrease in temperature with height. The relative humidity remains low at all levels, but increases above about 15,000 ft.

Although instruments alone can give an accurate picture of the temperature and humidity of the air, a rough idea can be formed from the reaction of plants, human beings and animals. When the relative humidity is very low, human beings, who are not used to such conditions, feel the effect on their skin and lips, which become parched and may sometimes even develop cracks. Plants droop or lose some of their leaves suddenly. The writer recalls an occasion in 1938 when he travelled from Adawso to Koforidua one morning in perfectly normal conditions, but by the time he returned in the early afternoon many of the trees along the road were drooping and all the leaves looked withered. What had happened was that the Harmattan had set in suddenly that morning and the high relative humidity of the morning under the influence of the monsoon air had been replaced by the low relative humidity of the north-east trades. The month was January.

The reaction of the human body to temperature and humidity is not quite so simple. Our bodily temperature is normally 98·4° Fahrenheit, but we can endure much higher temperatures provided the air is dry and the body can cool itself by means of perspiration. If, however, the air is moist as well, then this cooling process caused by perspiration cannot take place effectively, and we feel oppressed by the heat. On the other hand, if there is no change in the relative humidity we feel cold when the temperature drops or hot when it rises markedly above normal. But it must be remembered that the words 'hot' and 'cold' are relative terms, depending on what we have grown accustomed to in the place where we habitually live.

The chief characteristics of Ghana's climate are the relatively high temperatures felt in all places throughout the year, the great variation in the amount, duration and seasonal distribution of the rainfall from south to north, and the tendency of the dry seasons which separate the rainy seasons to grow longer and more intense with distance from the sea (Fig. 10). There are three important elements: temperature, rainfall and humidity.[1]

I. TEMPERATURE

With its northernmost part lying not more than $11\frac{1}{2}°$ from the equator and even less from the thermal equator, Ghana receives an abundant supply of warmth from the sun at all times of the year. Except for a few places where temperatures are reduced by high altitudes, the annual mean temperatures for the whole country range from 79° F. to 84° F. The lowest figures tend to occur near the coast and the highest further inland in the north.

Much greater than the difference between the lowest and the highest annual mean temperatures is the mean daily range of temperature, which is 12 or 13° F. near the coast and as much as 18–30° F. further inland (Table 2). One reason for the greater range inland is the rapid loss of heat at night due to radiation under comparatively clear skies and the absence of the sea, which moderates temperatures in the south during the day and helps to conserve heat at night.

Over the greater part of the country, the highest day or monthly mean maximum temperatures occur in March or February, whilst the lowest occur in August. The annual mean maximum temperature is greatest (94° F.) in the extreme north and least on the coast (85–6° F.). On the other hand the lowest night or monthly mean minimum temperatures occur in January or, along the coast, in August, whilst the highest temperatures are most commonly recorded in March, though they sometimes occur in April or May (Fig. 11).

Occasionally, certain places register temperatures much higher or lower than those mentioned above. For example, a temperature of 108° F. was once recorded at Navrongo in the Upper Region,

[1] See H. O. Walker, *Weather and Climate of Ghana*, Ghana Meteorological Service Note No. 5 (Accra, 1957).

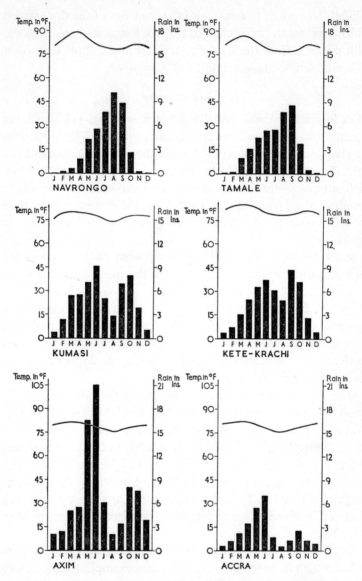

Fig. 10. Mean monthly distribution of temperature and rainfall
at selected stations.

28

Station		Jan.	Feb.	Mar.	Apr.	May	June	July	Aug.	Sept.	Oct.	Nov.	Dec.	Annual mean
Accra	Maximum	89·0	89·2	89·6	89·4	87·4	84·0	81·1	80·9	83·3	85·3	87·7	88·8	86·3
	Minimum	73·0	74·2	74·8	74·7	73·9	72·6	71·2	70·3	71·3	72·1	73·0	73·6	72·9
	Average	81·0	81·7	82·2	82·1	80·7	78·3	76·1	75·6	77·3	78·7	80·3	81·2	79·6
Axim	Maximum	86·0	87·3	88·2	88·0	86·3	83·2	81·7	80·5	81·4	83·6	86·6	87·0	84·9
	Minimum	74·1	74·8	75·7	75·6	74·7	73·9	73·5	72·2	73·0	73·7	73·0	73·7	74·0
	Average	80·0	81·0	81·9	81·8	80·5	78·5	77·6	76·3	77·2	78·6	79·8	80·3	79·4
Kumasi	Maximum	87·7	90·3	90·2	88·9	87·5	84·6	81·4	79·9	82·9	85·4	87·3	87·1	86·1
	Minimum	66·6	69·0	70·9	71·2	71·3	70·6	69·7	68·7	69·7	69·9	69·5	68·4	69·6
	Average	77·1	79·7	80·5	80·1	79·4	77·6	75·5	74·3	76·3	77·7	78·4	77·7	77·9
Kete-Krachi	Maximum	95·0	96·9	97·0	95·0	92·1	88·0	85·2	84·4	87·2	89·6	92·8	94·1	91·4
	Minimum	68·7	72·2	75·1	74·7	74·0	72·7	72·1	71·5	71·7	71·3	70·4	66·5	71·7
	Average	81·9	84·5	86·1	84·9	83·1	80·3	78·7	77·9	79·5	80·5	81·6	80·3	81·6
Tamale	Maximum	96·1	98·4	99·9	97·1	92·2	87·7	85·3	84·0	85·6	89·4	94·9	95·2	92·1
	Minimum	68·5	72·7	76·2	76·1	74·3	72·2	71·7	71·3	71·0	71·1	70·7	67·5	71·9
	Average	82·3	85·5	88·1	86·6	83·3	79·9	78·5	77·7	78·3	80·3	82·8	81·3	82·1
Navrongo	Maximum	95·8	99·1	102·0	101·3	96·6	90·8	87·3	85·2	87·0	92·1	96·7	95·4	94·1
	Minimum	66·3	71·3	75·6	78·1	77·1	73·7	72·5	72·1	71·5	71·5	68·1	65·2	71·9
	Average	81·1	85·2	88·8	89·7	86·9	82·3	79·9	78·7	79·3	81·8	82·4	80·3	83·0

Table. 2. *Mean monthly maximum and minimum temperatures and average daily means (degrees Fahrenheit*

whilst a temperature as low as 53° F. has been known to occur at both Kumasi and Tafo, in Ashanti and the Eastern Region respectively.

Generally speaking, high temperatures occur in February and March just before the onset of the rainy season, when the sun's

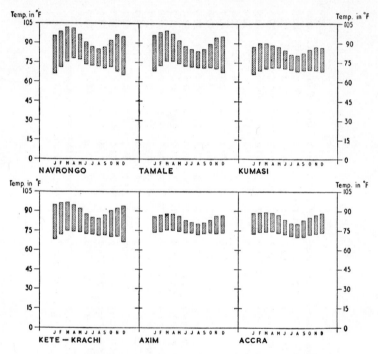

Fig. 11. Mean monthly range of temperature at selected stations.

rays reach the earth unimpeded during the day and the prevailing air mass is not of the 'cold' variety. The lowest temperatures at night occur in inland districts when the prevailing air mass is relatively cold and the skies are sufficiently clear to permit rapid radiation at night. January is therefore the month of low night temperatures here. Near the coast, where the influence of the Harmattan is not so strong, such conditions are found during the comparatively dry month of August, which is also the time when day temperatures are at their lowest owing to the prevalence of mist, which considerably reduces insolation. It has been suggested that the August mist is due to the effect of the Benguella current, which during this period brings its cold waters much closer to the Guinea coast than usual.

Apart from the effects of insolation and air masses on temperature, a number of local modifications are caused by the presence and distribution of high land. Temperatures normally fall about 3° F. for every thousand feet of ascent above sea-level, and thus places situated on high ground, such as the Akwapim-Togo Ranges, the Kwahu and Gambaga Plateaus and the isolated ranges found in the Akan Dissected Peneplain, have rather cooler conditions than their surrounding areas of lowland.

Even where the reduction in temperature is only 4 or 6° F., the human body quickly feels the difference, and it is not unusual in some of these places for people to sit round fires at night during the 'cold' part of the year. The writer recalls a bitterly cold night he experienced once at Akropong, Akwapim, although the temperature had only dropped to 65° F.

Areas of high land can also modify temperature by impeding the advance of winds. There is no doubt that but for the protection afforded by the Southern Voltaian Plateau, the Harmattan wind would penetrate much further south in January and cause a considerable fall in temperature in the forest country to the south.

2. RAINFALL

Rainfall in Ghana is largely the result of the interaction between the north-east trades or harmattan and the south-west winds or monsoon. It is the monsoon that brings the moist, warm air required for the formation of rain, but its meeting with the north-east trades promotes cooling and condensation, which are necessary before rain can form. The intense heating of the air during the day and the resulting convection also help to form rain. Such rain is described as *convectional rainfall*. Sometimes, the ascent of air needed to produce rain is caused by winds striking a hill or mountain range. This leads to *orographical rain*. Another

31

type of rain is the *line squall*, which is really the kind of rain caused when the two main air masses meet and the warmer one is forced to rise and produce rain owing to the cooler air mass undercutting it or thrusting itself underneath it and lifting it upwards.

What results during a line squall is a narrow belt of bad weather, characterized by a long line of low black clouds and a rapid rise in wind speed when the belt actually passes overhead. In addition to heavy rain there is plenty of thunder, lightning, and a rapid change in wind direction. Line squalls are not the same as tornadoes, and the latter term, which has a very special meaning, should never be employed for Ghana or any part of West Africa.

The highest rainfall occurs at Esiama, with over 86 in. per year, and diminishes gradually northwards to between 40 and 50 in. per year in the Northern Region. The only major departure from this general pattern is in the area lying south and east of a line between Cape Three Points and Ho, where the rainfall decreases to under 30 in. a year. This area, which lies in the region of Accra, forms a zone of exceptionally low rainfall along the whole of the Guinea coast (Fig. 12). Occasionally, annual totals greatly in excess of the average figures or well below them occur.

Like the amount, the distribution of rainfall during the year varies considerably. Four main types can be recognized as follows (Table 3):

(1) A single rainy season with monthly totals increasing slowly from March and reaching a peak in August or September, after which there is a sharp decrease. This type occurs north of a line running approximately through Wa and Salaga, and conditions there are well shown by Tamale and Navrongo.

(2) A single rainy season between March and October, with little variation between the monthly totals. This occurs south of the area described in (1) (above), and is bounded on the south by a line running through Kintampo and Hohoe. A typical station in this zone is Kete-Krachi.

(3) Two rainy seasons with the peaks occurring in May–June and October. The totals in each of these months are similar and the periods December–February and July–early September are

32

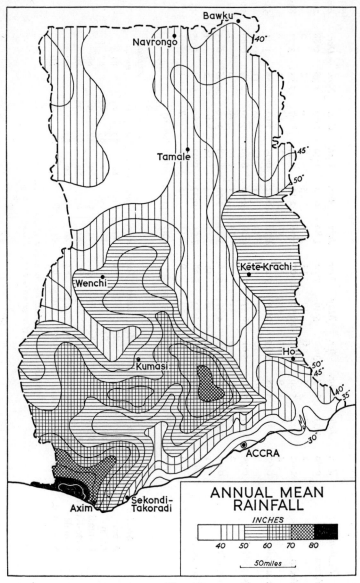

ANNUAL MEAN
RAINFALL

INCHES

40 50 60 70 80

50 miles

Fig. 12

33

Table 3. Mean monthly rainfall and number of rainy days (rainfall in inches)

Station	Jan.	Feb.	Mar.	Apr.	May	June	July	Aug.	Sept.	Oct.	Nov.	Dec.	Annual mean
Accra	0·59	1·33	2·27	3·40	5·46	7·10	1·80	0·58	1·40	2·63	1·38	0·88	28·82
	2	2	5	6	10	13	7	5	7	8	4	2	71
Axim	2·02	2·42	5·06	5·61	16·52	21·07	6·16	2·13	3·44	8·07	7·55	3·77	83·82
	4	5	9	11	18	19	11	9	12	14	13	8	133
Kumasi	0·67	2·31	5·38	5·65	7·15	9·21	4·96	2·92	6·95	7·94	3·86	1·21	58·21
	2	5	10	10	13	17	13	11	17	28	11	3	140
Kete-Krachi	0·75	1·47	3·22	5·01	6·57	7·54	6·20	4·90	8·76	7·30	2·69	0·86	55·27
	2	4	7	9	11	13	13	11	16	16	8	2	112
Tamale	0·09	0·29	2·03	3·25	4·67	5·66	5·69	7·70	8·78	3·76	0·56	0·15	42·63
	1	1	4	7	9	11	12	14	18	10	2	1	90
Navrongo	0·01	0·22	0·61	1·91	4·39	5·68	7·91	10·37	9·00	2·66	0·24	0·05	43·06
	1	1	1	4	7	9	11	15	15	7	1	1	73

Table 4. Mean monthly relative humidity at 0900 (9.00 a.m.)
G.M.T. (Greenwich Mean Time)

Station	Jan.	Feb.	Mar.	Apr.	May	June	July	Aug.	Sept.	Oct.	Nov.	Dec.	Annual mean
Accra	81	81	79	78	80	85	85	84	81	80	79	81	81
Axim	91	88	84	83	85	87	85	88	89	87	83	87	87
Kumasi	88	85	87	87	86	88	90	91	91	89	87	90	88
Kete-Krachi	74	68	73	76	80	85	87	85	87	86	82	78	80
Tamale	36	43	55	67	75	82	84	86	86	80	64	40	67
Navrongo	19	27	34	54	65	76	82	85	83	74	48	25	56

much drier than the rest of the year. This type occurs south of type (2) and is bounded on the south by a line through Wiawso and Keta. Its general features are well exemplified by Kumasi.

(4) Two rainy seasons, the principal one reaching its maximum in May and June and the subsidiary one in October. This type covers the whole of the coastal region. In the western section, which has the heaviest rainfall in the country, the May–June maximum is particularly well marked, whilst in the east the subsidiary season is much less pronounced. Conditions in the western section are well exemplified by Axim and those in the drier east by Accra.

3. HUMIDITY

The amount of water vapour present in a given volume of air at any time is very important from a climatic point of view, and is one of the factors which determine the behaviour of air masses and the resultant weather. It is usual, in discussing humidity, to distinguish between *absolute humidity* and *relative humidity*.

Absolute humidity is the actual amount of water vapour held at any particular time in a given volume of air. Relative humidity, on the other hand, means the fraction, expressed as a percentage, given by the amount of water vapour held in a given volume of air divided by the maximum amount that can be held at the same temperature and pressure.

Air which is near saturation point or has a relative humidity approaching 100 does not require much cooling before it yields its moisture either in the form of rain or in the form of dew. A plant surrounded by humid air is much less likely to lose its moisture and dry up than one which is surrounded by dry air. That is why forests tend to have comparatively humid conditions favourable to the growth of so many different kinds of plants forming the undergrowth. A great deal of the humidity found in them is derived from moisture transpired by the leaves of the trees themselves.

The southern part of Ghana is generally humid and relative humidities of 90–100 per cent are found on the coast during the night and early morning (Table 4). During the day humidity falls

35

to a minimum about noon, reaching 75 per cent in the south-west, where there is plenty of dense vegetation, and 65 per cent in the more open south-east. During the Harmattan in January the relative humidity can drop sharply in the south-east, and at Achimota figures as low as 12 per cent have been recorded.

Further inland the relative humidity is about 65 per cent, varying to the extent of 20 per cent above or below this figure during certain seasons. Here again, quite sharp changes can take place in the relative humidity, depending on whether the prevailing air mass is the monsoon or the north-east trades.

In the north there is a humid season from April to October, when night relative humidities may average 95 per cent, falling to 70 per cent during the afternoons. The remainder of the year is much drier. Average night relative humidities are about 80 per cent, falling to as low as 25 per cent in Navrongo during January.

The relative humidity is important for three main reasons: (1) It determines the ability of the air to form rain. (2) It controls the rate at which plants and animals lose their moisture. (3) It controls to a large extent the rate at which water bodies and the soil itself lose their water. This last consideration is of great significance in planning irrigation works and storage dams and in considering the use of mechanized farming, which involves the clearing and ploughing of large tracts of land, particularly in dry areas such as northern Ghana or the Accra Plains.

4. THE SEASONS

Places on the poleward sides of the tropics have clearly marked seasons, characterized by differences between the length of day and night and the amount of warmth reaching them from the sun. The warm part of the year is called *summer* and the cold part is called *winter*. As summer gives way to winter there is a transition season, varying in length according to the latitude, which is known as *autumn*, and as winter is replaced by summer there is another transition period known as *spring*. Autumn is the time when trees begin to lose their leaves because of the cold, and in America that

36

season is aptly known as the *fall*. During spring the plants, which were bare in winter, begin to flower and grow new leaves.

Ghana lies so close to the equator that such a division of the year is unsuitable on the grounds of temperature, which varies little throughout the year. The only significant division of the year here is into *rainy seasons* and *dry seasons*. It is pointless to use the terms winter, spring, summer and autumn in connection with the climate of Ghana.

During the rainy season and the period immediately following it, plants look fresh and green and the ground is easily worked for cultivation. On the other hand, during the dry season everything looks parched and hungry, and the green tints of the rainy season are replaced by brownish tints. The ground becomes hard, and soils containing much clay develop wide cracks. Roads are very dusty and the vegetation on either side becomes covered with thick layers of dust. During the Harmattan the dust-laden air makes the atmosphere hazy and thin films of dust settle on everything, including furniture. Although the dry season enables recently cleared bush and the grass to dry before burning and helps cocoa beans to dry properly, it can do a great deal of harm to valuable crops of food if it lasts too long.

4

RIVER SYSTEMS AND LAKES

Ghana is drained by a large number of streams and rivers forming a close network over most parts of the country. In addition to these are several coastal lagoons, the vast Lake Volta and one large inland lake, Bosumtwi, which has no outlet to the sea. It is in the wetter southern and south-western parts of the country that the stream network is closest. In the Accra coastal plains, Brong-Ahafo and northern Ghana, it is much less close (Fig. 13).

Not all these streams flow throughout the year. Even in the wettest areas all the smaller streams dry up or shrink very considerably at the height of the dry season, but quickly come back to life during the wet. This abundance of streams is one reason why road-building and maintenance are so expensive. Every little stream requires a proper culvert or bridge in order to enable vehicles to use the roads running across it throughout the year, and many culverts and bridges are destroyed during exceptionally heavy rains by the downrush of water.

Although rainfall makes a direct contribution to streams during the wet seasons, it is mainly from springs that most water bodies are fed. The formation of springs depends closely on the local geology and relief. Water is able to percolate fairly easily through certain types of rocks which are porous, e.g. sandstones, because the grains of the rock are not too closely cemented together, or pervious, because even though they may be closely grained they are broken up by large cracks or joints. But there are other rocks, such as clay, which are impermeable and do not permit the easy passage of water. When underground water meets an impermeable layer or mass it runs downwards along it, and if its journey brings it to the surface again at a convenient point such as the foot or side of a hill it issues out as a spring. A high water table aids the formation of springs.

38

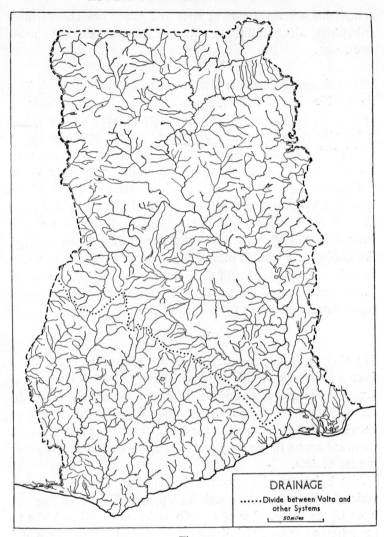

Fig. 13

With the exception of a small number which enter land-locked lakes like Bosumtwi or dry up inland, all streams and rivers in Ghana eventually empty themselves into the sea. Each river entering the sea can be looked upon as an independent system

39

comprising a main stream or river and minor branches forming tributaries, which in their turn may be fed by smaller tributaries, and so on.

DRAINAGE PATTERNS

The drainage of Ghana is dominated by the Volta system. This river, which was given its name by the Portuguese in the fifteenth century on account of its tortuous character, has a total length of some 1000 miles and drains an area of 150,000 square miles, of which 61,000 lie within Ghana. This means that as much as 67 per cent of the area of the country lies within the basin of the Volta.

Practically all the streams and rivers north and east of the Southern Voltaian Scarp between Sunyani and Koforidua form part of the Volta system. The Kwahu or Southern Voltaian Plateau is thus the most important river divide in the country. South of it are a number of smaller river systems draining directly into the sea. The largest of these are the Pra, Ankobra and the Tano, but some of the smaller ones are of considerable local significance as sources of water supply.

(a) The Volta

The Volta is an international river. It begins as the Black Volta from a low range of hills a few miles west of Bobo Dioulasso in Upper Volta and after flowing for about 200 miles in a north-easterly direction bends southwards to form the boundary between northern Ghana and the Ivory Coast. Near Bole it turns eastward across the country and then bends south again to enter the sea at Ada.

Just before turning south it is joined by the White Volta, which flows southward through the Upper and Northern Regions from Upper Volta. One of the tributaries of the White Volta in the extreme north-east of Ghana is the Red Volta. Like the White Volta and the Black Volta, this also rises in Upper Volta. Below the confluence of the Black and White Voltas, which is some 290 miles from the sea, the river is known as the Volta. In this section it has two major tributaries, the Oti, entering it from the north, and the Afram, from the west.

Although the Volta has the common West African characteristic of being interrupted by rapids at several points, notably in the region of the Ajena gorge, where it crosses the Akwapim-Togo Ranges, it has on the whole a very gentle gradient. The average gradient of the Black Volta is 2 ft. per mile, and that of the Volta proper for the last 290 miles of its course is only 1 ft. per mile.

Apart from its great length, the Volta is very wide. At Ada, where it enters the sea, the mouth is about a mile wide. But it is constantly shifting and has a bar which makes navigation difficult. Small coastal steamers can, however, enter, and the river is navigable for steam launches and lighters all the year round to Akuse, which is the tidal limit, although there is very little of this traffic nowadays. In the rainy season navigation can be continued further, up to the Senchi rapids five miles north of Kpong, but beyond this, until the creation of Lake Volta, only canoe traffic was possible on account of the numerous rapids, of which the most dangerous were at Kete-Krachi. At Yeji, where the Great North Road from Kumasi to Tamale crosses the river, the width is about 600 yards.

Except at the height of the dry season, all the Voltas flow perennially, or at least have pools of water in their beds. Motor vehicles cross by ferries at Yeji, Bamboi, Tefle and Kete-Krachi. Until the opening of the bridge at Adomi (Plate 1), a few miles north of Senchi, early in 1957, no bridge crossed the Volta proper. This bridge has now replaced the ferry at Senchi. Another bridge under construction at Tefle will provide a direct road link between Ghana and its eastern neighbours.

The Volta contains large reserves of potential power which could be harnessed to serve the needs of the people of Ghana. So far all this power has run to waste year after year, but under the Volta River Aluminium Scheme a dam has been constructed at Akosombo to generate hydro-electric power for the production of aluminium from bauxite, of which the country has large reserves.

The construction of the Akosombo dam has created a large reservoir of water with an area of 3500 square miles extending over 200 miles upstream to a little beyond the confluence of the

Black and White Voltas. This will add considerably to the existing means of communication between the northern and southern parts of Ghana and provide an important source of fish.

The regime of the Volta depends closely on the rainfall regime of its basin. As this lies further north than those of other river systems in the country the season of the highest floods is somewhat delayed, occurring between August and December, whereas floods in the more southerly rivers occur between May and October. There is a marked difference between the flow of the Volta during the dry season and during the flood season. In the former period the banks may stand as much as 20–50 ft. above the water, but during the latter season they stand only 8–12 ft. above it and sometimes the water completely overflows its banks and rushes down with a strong current. These differences are also reflected in the rate of flow of the river. In the section below the gorge it varies from under 1000 cusecs. (cu. ft. per sec.) during the dry season to between 125,000 and 390,000 cusecs. during the flood period.

(b) The Pra

The Pra river and its tributaries, the Ofin, the Anum and the Birim, form the largest river system draining the Akan Dissected Peneplain. The Pra itself takes its source from the Kwahu section of the Southern Voltaian Plateau, not far from Mpraeso, but the Ofin and the Anum come from much further north, in the area between Mampong and Effiduase in Ashanti. The Birim is more southerly. It rises not far from Kibi in the Atewa-Atwiredu Range and flows northward. At Anyinam it bends back on itself through the Anyinam gap and finally joins the Pra west of Oda (Fig. 35).

The Pra enters the sea a few miles east of Shama. Six miles inland at Beposo it is crossed by a magnificent suspension bridge which carries the motor road between Accra and Takoradi. The Pra is seriously hampered by rapids and even small canoes can only use short sections of it. One of the worst sections is the one between Anyinabrim and Krobo, where the Bosomasi rapids occur. Canoes sometimes cross these rapids, but those who have made the venture know how perilous it is.

Although the Pra is of little use for navigation, in the early part of this century both the main river and the Ofin were used a great deal for floating down timber from the forest region to the coast for export. Today all the timber from the basin finds its way to the port of Takoradi or other places by road and rail. Just as the Volta forms an international and inter-regional boundary, so also the Pra over a large section of its course marks the boundary between Ashanti and the Eastern Region. It played a notable part in many of the wars of bygone centuries between the Akims and other armies of the south on the one hand and the Ashantis on the other.

(c) The Ankobra

The Ankobra lies to the west of the Pra. It is a much smaller river and its basin is confined almost entirely to the Western Region of Ghana. Although it contains rapids in its upper reaches, the lower section is navigable for some 50 miles from its mouth by steam launches. Indeed, from 1877 until the construction of the Sekondi-Tarkwa railway in 1901 all the heavy machinery employed in the Tarkwa gold-mining industry was transported by canoes from the mouth of the Ankobra as far as Tomento, whence it was conveyed to Tarkwa by head porterage. One remarkable feature of the Ankobra is that its lower section as far as Tomento is tidal, and the water rises and falls about 2 ft. between high and low tide.

The chief tributaries of the Ankobra are the Mansi and the Bonsa. The headwaters of both of them come remarkably close to the Pra system. It has been suggested that the lower Bonsa, which flows from east to west, has captured the upper Bonsa, which probably once flowed directly into the sea along a north–south course. This can only be one of several examples of river capture to be found in Ghana. Apart from the question of capture, the lower Bonsa is of considerable interest because its course closely follows the general direction of a series of short faults.

(d) The Tano

The Tano is the westernmost river of Ghana, and just before entering the broad Aby Lagoon in the south-east corner of the

Ivory Coast marks the international boundary between the two countries. The river takes its rise not far from Techiman to the north-west of Kumasi and follows an almost direct southerly course towards the sea. It is navigable for steam launches as far as Tanosu, above which the Sutre Falls make further navigation impossible, except locally on a small scale.

(e) The minor coastal streams

In addition to these four large river systems are a number of smaller ones which are of importance only in the areas they traverse. They are usually short, and the most significant ones occur between the Pra and the Volta. Typical ones are the Ayensu, which enters the sea near Winneba, and the Densu, which reaches the sea through the Sakumo Lagoon a few miles west of Accra. The pipe-borne water supply of Accra is derived from the Densu and that of Winneba from the Ayensu.

(f) Lake Bosumtwi[1]

This lake, lying 21 miles south-east of Kumasi, is the only real lake in Ghana. It is believed that the cavity which it occupies was formed when the top of a volcano blew off and therefore provides an example of a CALDERA LAKE. But there is another theory which suggests that the depression occupied by the lake was formed when a meteorite struck the earth. It has an area of about $18\frac{1}{2}$ square miles and is between 230 and 240 ft. deep. Above the level of the lake the sides rise steeply from 500 to 1400 ft., and several small streams flow down into the lake, though there is no drainage leading out of it. Lake Bosumtwi has considerable wealth in fish, but as it is regarded as sacred by the Ashantis the fish are not available for general exploitation. The lake attracts considerable numbers of tourists on account of its scenic beauty.

(g) The coastal lagoons

There are several lagoons along the coast, particularly west of Cape Three Points and east of Accra. Most of them are really the

[1] See *Gold Coast Geological Survey Bulletin No. 8* (1937), 'The Geology of the Bosumtwi Caldera and Surrounding Country'.

mouths of rivers, which have been ponded back by the sea, and are separated from the sea by a low sand-bar. At low tide the bar is above water, but during high tide the sea flows easily over the bar and enters the lagoons, whose waters are therefore almost invariably brackish.

It is likely that the formation of lagoons has been helped considerably by the periodic elevation of the land above the sea during recent geological times, but perhaps an even greater factor is the strong south-west wind, which sets up a great swell or long-shore drift capable of transporting large quantities of sand along the coast to block the mouths of the rivers. Owing to the absence of powerful tides along the coast and the gentle slope of the river mouths, there is no force strong enough to remove such accumulations of sand.

5

VEGETATION AND SOILS

I. VEGETATION

Vegetation is a collective name for plants. A distinction is usually made between natural vegetation and man-made vegetation. Natural vegetation refers to those plants which have not been deliberately planted by man, while man-made vegetation, as the name implies, is vegetation which has been planted specially by man. Such things as farm and plantation crops and plants grown for ornamental purposes are all part of the man-made vegetation.

Vegetation is determined largely by the soil and climatic conditions. However, owing to man's ability, within certain limits, to create special conditions for plants which he wants to grow, the man-made vegetation does not always reflect soil and climatic conditions as faithfully as does the natural vegetation. Even the natural vegetation may be affected in important ways by man's activities, which may be helpful, or harmful and destructive. In addition to present-day physical conditions, the past history of an area and the various conditions which have prevailed there for the establishment or destruction of different types of plants also affect the character of the natural vegetation.

This section will be concerned with the natural vegetation. As temperatures throughout Ghana are always high enough to promote plant growth, the distribution of the natural vegetation depends primarily on the amount of rainfall and the length of the dry season. Here and there, particularly in swampy areas, soils also have an effect on the vegetation.

Four broad vegetation types are distinguished in Ghana.[1] These are: (*a*) high forest, (*b*) savanna-woodland, (*c*) coastal scrub and

[1] See C. J. Taylor, *The Vegetation Zones of the Gold Coast* (Government Printer, Accra, 1953).

grassland, and (*d*) strand and mangrove (Fig. 14*a*). Except in the case of the strand and mangrove vegetation, the boundaries between the different zones are rarely precise. One type merges gradually into the next, producing an intermediate type,[1] and frequently outliers of one type may be found in another. This is often due to the presence of mountains and rivers or other special circumstances. Most rivers, even when they run through the dry savanna region, are fringed with gallery forests, on account of the moisture along their banks, and mountains may also have a wooded or grassy appearance in the midst of open or generally forested country.

(*a*) *High forest*

With the exception of a narrow coastal belt extending from 10 to 20 miles between Takoradi and Ada, the high forest occupies the whole of the south-west part of Ghana south of the northern scarp of the Southern Voltaian Plateau and west of the eastern edge of the Akwapim Ranges. It covers an area of approximately 25,000 square miles. Across the Volta, the Togo section of the Ranges forms an outlier of the high forest.

The annual rainfall varies from over 85 in. along the coast to 50 in. along the inland boundaries of this area, and the other climatic characteristics are roughly similar to those of types 3 and 4 described under 'Rainfall' in chapter 3.

The high forest is made up of a large variety of plants, which are arranged in a series of well-marked layers or STOREYS. Near the ground, especially on the edges of the forest, in open spaces, or along footpaths, where the sunlight penetrates to the ground, are found small herbs, shrubs and grasses. At a height of 60 ft. occurs the second storey made up of trees with low branches and heavy crowns. Above this comes the upper storey formed by trees with tall, straight stems, usually with small crowns forming a closed canopy about 130 ft. high. Lastly are the very tall trees reaching up to 200 ft. They are scattered and do not form a closed canopy. Entwined through the trees are lianes, some of which go right up to the tops of the highest trees.

---

[1] Botanists refer to such intermediate vegetation types as *ecotones*.

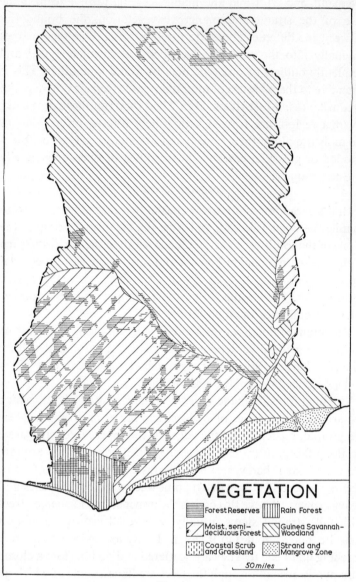

VEGETATION

Forest Reserves

Rain Forest

Moist, semi-deciduous Forest

Guinea Savannah-Woodland

Coastal Scrub and Grassland

Strand and Mangrove Zone

50 miles

Fig. 14a

48

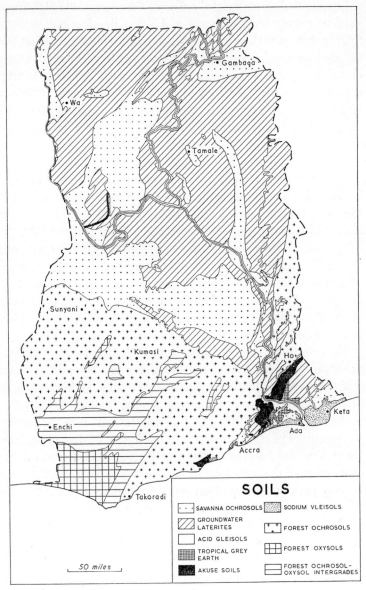

SOILS

- ⋯ SAVANNA OCHROSOLS
- ▨ GROUNDWATER LATERITES
- ☐ ACID GLEISOLS
- ▦ TROPICAL GREY EARTH
- ■ AKUSE SOILS
- ⣿ SODIUM VLEISOLS
- ✛ FOREST OCHROSOLS
- ▦ FOREST OXYSOLS
- ☐ FOREST OCHROSOL-OXYSOL INTERGRADES

50 miles

Fig. 14b

Despite their great height, many of the trees in the high forest have extremely shallow roots and often develop buttresses at their base to give them additional support. This and the fact that the various species are usually widely scattered in small stands make the economic exploitation of the forest difficult. It takes considerable time and trouble to find particular types of timber, and before felling can take place it is often necessary to erect a platform so as to reach the trunk of the tree above the buttresses at the base (Plate 8).

Within the high forest two subdivisions are usually recognized: the *rain forest* and the *moist semi-deciduous forest*. The rain forest is found in the extreme south-west corner of the country, where the annual rainfall ranges from 65 to 86 in., the relative humidity is very high and there is practically no month without rain.

The trees of the rain forest are evergreen for the most part, and only a few in the two uppermost storeys shed their leaves, or, in other words, show deciduous characteristics. But even such trees do not all shed their leaves at the same time, and the appearance of the forest therefore changes very little from one part of the year to another.

The rain forest does not extend much further north of Prestea or east of Dixcove. The rest of the high forest is made up of the moist semi-deciduous forest. The annual rainfall in this area varies between 50 and 65 in. The relative humidity is also much less than in the rain forest, and the effect of the Harmattan much greater.

The structure of this forest is very similar to that of the rain forest, the main difference lying in the fact that a much larger proportion of the trees here have deciduous characteristics. For varying periods between October and April several trees in the two uppermost storeys lose their leaves. As in the rain forest the trees do not all shed their leaves at once, and the forest is therefore never completely barren of leaves in the same way that the true deciduous forests of temperate latitudes are during winter. That is why the description 'semi-deciduous' rather than just 'deciduous' is given to them. A remarkable feature about the moist semi-deciduous forest is that while the trees in the lower storey are usually evergreen, taller members of the same species in the higher storeys may be deciduous.

Owing to its large extent and differences in climatic conditions, the character of the semi-deciduous forest changes gradually from south to north. There is a decrease in the luxuriance of the forest as the rainfall decreases and the effect of the Harmattan increases. In the extreme north and east where it adjoins the Guinea savanna-woodland much destruction has been caused to it by fire in connection with hunting and farming, and there are signs that the forest is gradually giving way to savanna-woodland.

Not all the area described as having a forest vegetation is in fact covered by forest. Farming operations over the years have destroyed large parts, and the vegetation found today on areas that are not under cultivation is only a temporary CLIMAX consisting of secondary bush. The trees here may be of low or high stature, according to the length of time during which they have been left untouched by man. Given a very long period of recovery, secondary bush can return to something closely approaching the original vegetation cover (Plate 2a), but owing to the increasing pressure on agricultural land, such long periods of rest are impossible today. Two years, or at most ten years, is the period during which most farmed land is nowadays allowed to revert to bush before it is cleared again for cultivation, and it is reckoned that farming destroys about 300 square miles of forest every year.[1]

Most of the areas of true forest are to be found in the 5882 square miles of forest reserves, where cultivation and the indiscriminate extraction of timber are forbidden by the government. Apart from the conservation of useful timber, an important function of these forest reserves is to act as shelter belts against the dry Harmattan winds from the north and also to protect the headwaters of streams.

(b) Savanna-woodland

The savanna-woodland, sometimes called the Guinea savanna-woodland, is the most extensive vegetation type (Plate 23 a and b).

[1] See D. Kinloch and W. A. Miller, *Gold Coast Timbers*, Government Printing Department (Takoradi, 1949).

With an area of about 65,000 square miles, it covers the whole of the region north of the high forest. In its typical form it is composed of short trees, often widely spaced, with a more or less continuous carpet of grass. Some of the grasses attain a height of about 12 ft.

Most of the area lies within the zone which has one rainy season occurring in August–September, although along the south the regime approaches that of the high forest. Although the annual rainfall rarely falls below 40 or 50 in., the dry season is very intense and imposes a limit on the vegetation. From November to April, when the Harmattan is blowing, the relative humidity is extremely low. The intense aridity of the dry season causes the soil to become very hard, and much of the rain which falls at the beginning of the rainy season runs off the hard-baked soil before it is properly absorbed by the vegetation.

The trees show a marked adaptation to the environment. Many of them are fire-resistant and have thick barks. Trees like baobabs and the shea tree (*Butyrospermum parkii*) as well as several types of acacia are well adapted to withstand the long drought and strong, desiccating winds by their shiny or hairy leaves and their umbrella-shaped crowns, which present only a thin edge to the wind.

Here, too, the hand of man has left its mark on the vegetation. Along the south the savanna is really 'derived' from what was formerly high forest, while in the extreme north-east of the country, north of the Gambaga Scarp, the marked absence of trees is due to the extensive destruction of the natural vegetation caused by human settlement and continual burning and cultivation by a comparatively dense population.

(c) Coastal scrub and grassland

This vegetation zone extends as a narrow strip from near Takoradi and widens towards the east to about 20 miles in the vicinity of Keta. The rainfall is very low, averaging 33 in. or even as low as 28 in. near Accra.

The vegetation consists either of dense scrub with hardly any grass, such as is found in the western section of the zone, or else of grassland studded with clumps of bush and patches of scrub (Plate 2*b*), with here and there a few characteristic trees such as baobabs (*Adansonia digitata*) and *Elaeophorbia drupifera*. The commonest type of grass is Guinea grass (*Panicum maximum*). In the moister western parts and also in the extreme east, fan palms are common, and also the oil palm (*Elaeis guineensis*).

The section east of Weija is commonly known as the Accra Plains (Plates 2*b* and 3*a*). Altogether it is more open than the section to the west, which forms the Cape Coast–Winneba Plains (Plate 3*b*) and baobabs and fleshy-leaved euphorbias, particularly *Elaeophorbia drupifera*, are more common. An even more striking feature of the Accra Plains is the abundance of termite mounds. They are particularly abundant in the drier section within 10 miles of the sea. Some of them form tall pinnacles, up to 10 ft. high, with fluted sides, but large numbers have broken down and occur as large, circular mounds, frequently covered by a thick growth of shrubs and trees.

(*d*) Strand and mangrove

This type of vegetation is almost confined to the immediate coastal area, both along the sea front and in the beds of lagoons. Along the sea shore the vegetation is constantly bathed in sea-spray and surrounded by the moist sea breeze. The plant cover does not form a continuous carpet, but consists rather of succulent erect or creeping herbs, tufted plants and grasses, which bind the sand with long, spring-like shoots on partly buried horizontal stems.

The lagoons and the beds of old lagoons, which are under water during the rains, are mainly associated with mangroves. These mangroves are not very extensive and do not form big trees. In the stagnant sections of lagoons a number of water plants may be found.

2. SOILS

Soils are the joint product of rocks, climate and vegetation. The rocks provide the parent material, while the vegetation provides the all-important organic substances which give the soil the characteristics that distinguish it from rock waste or sand. The

53

climate determines the processes to which the soil is exposed and the factors that are mainly responsible for breaking up the rock initially into small enough particles for soil formation. Another factor affecting the formation and distribution of soils is topography, and in areas having the same geological and climatic conditions it has been found that there is generally a regular pattern of change in soil characteristics, from the hill-tops, through the valley sides, to the valleys themselves.

On the whole the main rock types found in Ghana show marked resemblances to each other, both as regards their great age and also as regards the presence in all of them of considerable proportions of quartz. Quartz is the material from which sand is commonly formed, and it is the parent material of the Voltaian sandstones, as of the quartzites of the Akwapim-Togo Ranges. It also forms an important constituent of both the Tarkwaian and Birrimian rocks and the granitic intrusions in the rest of the country.

Because of this fundamental similarity in the rocks of the country, it is largely climate, vegetation, topography and drainage that determine differences in soil types. The soil is subject to two main processes due to climate. The percolation or downward movement of rain water tends to dissolve the mineral constituents and carry them downwards. Working in the opposite direction, the heat of the sun sets up capillary attraction through evaporation, and this brings up a number of salts in solution and deposits them as a hard pan near the surface.

Where the rainfall and insolation are both moderate these two processes are kept in balance, but where one or other predominates, the soil is either completely leached or else rendered of little use for cultivation owing to the hard pan near the surface with its excess of salts and other chemical compounds. Other factors affecting soils in Ghana are the great humidity and heat, which speed up chemical processes in the soil and cause organic matter to decay very rapidly, thus losing its value after a very short time. As soon as the supply of fresh humus is delayed or cut off completely the soils begin to deteriorate in fertility.

The source of all this humus is the vegetation. But in addition to providing humus the vegetation performs the important function of providing a cover for the soil and protecting it against leaching, evaporation and erosion. It is this kind of protection which the forest and secondary bush give land that is not under cultivation. A similar kind of protection is given by crops growing on cultivated land. If such land were to be exposed for long without adequate vegetation cover the soil would be destroyed very quickly. It is thought that the great dependence of soils in Ghana on plant humus for most of their plant nutrients is due largely to the fact that most of the rocks are composed of materials deposited on land and have undergone such prolonged weathering since that they have lost most of their potential plant foods. Ghana is not exceptional in this respect; the same thing can be said of soils in almost all other parts of tropical Africa.

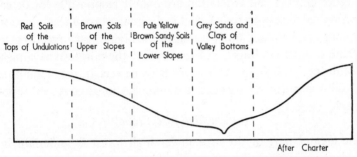

| Red Soils of the Tops of Undulations | Brown Soils of the Upper Slopes | Pale Yellow Brown Sandy Soils of the Lower Slopes | Grey Sands and Clays of Valley Bottoms |

After Charter

Fig. 15. A typical catena in the cocoa-growing zone of Ghana.

The changes which occur repeatedly in the soil as a result of topography and drainage conditions are known as *soil catenas*[1] (Fig. 15). Usually soils found on hill-tops have developed directly from the underlying rock, and are therefore described as *residual* or *sedentary* soils. On the other hand, the soils found in valleys and on the lower hill slopes have usually been brought down from elsewhere and are therefore known as *transported* soils.

Soils may also be described as stony, sandy, silty or clayey according to the texture of the mineral grains composing them. Where the particles are very fine the soil is described as clayey,

[1] See *Journal of Ecology*, vol. xxxv (1947), p. 192, J. Milne.

whilst increasingly larger particles give it a silty to sandy character and so on until stones are reached. The water-retaining qualities of the soil and therefore its usefulness for agriculture depend closely on the soil particles. Clayey soils tend to be unsuitable for agriculture. During wet seasons they become waterlogged, while during dry seasons they lose their water quickly and shrink, thus producing large cracks in many cases. On the other hand, sandy soils permit the passage of water so easily that they quickly dry up when the supply ceases. The best soils for farming consist of a combination of sand, silt and clay. This permits the soil to retain an adequate supply of moisture without the danger of becoming waterlogged during the wet season or parched during the dry. Such soils are known as *loams*, and depending on the preponderance of clay or sand one can speak of *heavy loams* or *sandy loams*.

Since climate and vegetation are mainly responsible for determining differences in soils found in Ghana, a broad classification of soils can be made into (*a*) soils of the high forest zone, (*b*) soils of the coastal savannas, and (*c*) soils of the northern savannas. Within each of these main types may be recognized a number of sub-types due to significant differences in geology and topography (Fig. 14*b*).

(a) The high forest zone[1]

The greater part of the area under high forest is underlain by ancient rocks containing considerable proportions of quartzite and comprising granites and gneisses over large areas. With the exception of the highland rims on the north and east, this part of Ghana consists of a series of old, dissected peneplains giving rise to a gently undulating topography. Although the rainfall here is quite heavy (between 45 and 86 in. per annum) the vegetation cover prevents excessive leaching during the wet season and excessive evaporation during the Harmattan.

The surface soil generally has a light texture and a grey-brown or brown colour. It is rich in humus and worm-casts, which give it its dark colour. Below it is a reddish brown zone, 2 or 3 ft. thick, containing ironstone concretions which give it its reddish

[1] See C. F. Charter, *Report of Cocoa Conference* (London, 1949), pp. 105–12.

colour. These ironstone concretions are formed in this zone as a result of the concentration of iron-containing solutions during dry periods. With the concretions is mixed quartz gravel derived from the numerous quartz veins to be found in the rocks. But for the constant activity of earthworms, termites and other soil organisms which add to the topsoil, the zone of ironstone concretions and quartz gravel would soon be uncovered. Finally, down to a depth of up to 10 ft. is a lower zone of clayey, rotten rock, pale greyish yellow to grey and mottled reddish or orange in its upper part, resting on little-weathered rock.

The nearness of the bedrock to the surface is of great importance to the fertility of the soil, for it means that the rock minerals which on decomposition give rise to plant foods are within easy reach of the roots of plants.

Where the proportion of quartz in the rocks is high, as in predominantly sandstone or quartzite areas, the soils have a paler colour, usually yellowish or brownish, and are not particularly fertile in themselves.

The forest soils of Ghana fall into two principal groups known as *ochrosols* and *oxysols*. The ochrosols are found in the area where the rainfall ranges between 65 and 45 in. per annum, while the oxysols occur in the wetter southern part, where the rainfall ranges from 70 to 85 in. per annum.

The *ochrosols* are usually red or reddish brown on the summits and upper slopes of hills, orange-brown or brown on the middle slopes, and yellow-brown on the lower slopes. They are generally better drained and less acidic than the oxysols and cover a much larger area of the forest. From an agricultural point of view, they form the most important soils in the forest zone as well as in the entire country, since they support practically all the cocoa and many of the most widely consumed food crops.

In contrast, the *oxysols*, which cover a relatively small area, are very highly leached, owing to the heavy rainfall, and tend to be more acidic and less rich in humus than the ochrosols. They are also paler in colour, ranging from orange-brown to yellow-brown on summits and upper slopes. Agriculturally, their use seems to be rather limited, but the very heavy rainfall appears to favour the cultivation of such tree crops as rubber, oil palm and bananas.

In the area with a rainfall of between 65 and 75 in. per annum, both ochrosols and oxysols are found, and the soils here are accordingly referred to as *ochrosol–oxysol intergrades*.

(b) The coastal savannas

The chief differences between this zone and the preceding one lie in the lower rainfall and the greater exposure of the soil to evaporation owing to the comparatively thin vegetation cover.

Much of this area was stripped of its former soil cover by erosion during Quaternary times, and the present soils are therefore much younger and show a more direct relationship with the underlying rocks than in other parts of the country. The termites, which abound in this zone, also appear to have played a major role in soil formation by transferring to the surface material from the weathered rock below. Consequently, many of the soils are referred to as *drift soils*.

Owing to the varied geology of the area, several soil types are found, of which the principal ones are the *savanna ochrosols*, the *groundwater laterites* and the *tropical black earths* or *Akuse soils* Other soils are the *tropical grey earths*, the *acid gleisols* and the *sodium vleisols*.

The *savanna ochrosols* are formed on the Tertiary deposits bordering the Volta delta. They are well-drained, friable and porous loams ranging in colour from red to yellow-brown and are the most fertile and easily cultivated soils in the coastal zone. The *groundwater laterites*, which are formed on the acidic gneisses, consist of pale-coloured sand of varying thickness, lying on top of a mottled, gravelly sandy clay, which in turn is underlain by weathered acidic gneiss or granite. Because of the underlying clay, this soil has poor drainage during the wet season and is consequently not very useful for agriculture. The *tropical black earths* are found on the basic gneisses, which extend as a fairly broad band north-eastwards across the plains from Tema. They are dark-coloured, heavy clays with a poorly developed profile, which become extremely soggy during the wet season but develop wide cracks during the dry season. One of their principal characteristics is the high proportion of lime which they contain and which forms conspicuous concretions. Unlike most other soils in this zone, these soils are highly alkaline. Owing to their heavy nature and the cracks which they develop during the dry season there is little cultivation on them at present, but experiments have shown that they are potentially fertile, given the right crops and suitable methods of cultivation.

The other soils are not of much use for cultivation. The *tropical grey earths* occur on the southern section of the acidic gneiss zone east of the black earths. Like the groundwater laterites, they are underlain by a clayey hardpan which impedes drainage, thus making cultivation difficult. Their principal use is to provide grazing grounds for cattle. The *acid gleisols* are associated with the alluvial deposits along the Volta below Kpong. They consist mostly of clays and support little cultivation. The *sodium vleisols* are found on the recent deposits along the brackish lagoons and creeks of the Volta Delta as well as around the other lagoons along the coast.

(c) The northern savannas

The northern savannas are underlain largely by Voltaian rocks, but in the extreme west and north occur wide expanses of granite, associated with the older crystalline complex of the Wa-Navrongo-Bawku dissected peneplain.

Although the rainfall here is considerably heavier and the vegetation much thicker generally than in the coastal savannas, the dry season is far more intense than in any other part of the country, with the result that the soil is exposed to alternate leaching and evaporation. The effect of the leaching is to remove valuable nutrients, while that of the intense evaporation is to promote the formation of a hard pan composed mainly of ironstone concretions near the surface, especially in the areas underlain by Voltaian sandstones.

In general the soils of this zone are very much poorer in organic matter and plant nutrients than the forest soils, and their use for

59

cultivation is often further impeded by the low effective rainfall and its unreliability.

Two broad groups of soils are recognized in this zone: The *savanna ochrosols* and the *groundwater laterites*. In addition, acid gleisols are found on the alluvia bordering the Black and White Voltas and their larger tributaries.

The *savanna ochrosols* are found on the Voltaian sandstones and the Tarkwaian and Lower Birrimian rocks. They consist of well-drained, friable, porous loams and are mostly red or reddish brown in colour. Most of the area covered by these soils has a gently undulating topography. Soils in the depressions are quite thick, but upland soils usually have a zone of ironstone concretions from one to three feet below the surface. Despite their deficiency in nutrients, notably phosphorus and nitrogen, these soils are among the best soils in the northern savanna zone and are extensively farmed. The former Gonja Development Company's farm at Damongo is situated on these soils.

The *groundwater laterites* are very extensive and are formed on the Voltaian shales and the granites. They consist of a pale-coloured, sandy or silty loam with a depth of up to 2 ft. underlain by an ironpan or a mottled clayey layer so rich in iron that it hardens to form an ironpan on exposure. Drainage on these soils is poor; they tend to get waterlogged during the rains and to dry out during the long dry season. These soils, especially those developed on the Voltaian shales, are considered to be among the poorest soils in Ghana, and little cultivation takes place on them. Their principal use is, and is likely to remain, the provision of rather poor pastures for livestock. Even so, careful conservation measures are essential on them, as they are highly susceptible to erosion.

NOTE. For a fuller treatment of soils, see *Agriculture and Land Use in Ghana*, edited by J. B. Wills, Oxford University Press, 1962.

PART II

HUMAN RESPONSE

6

AGRICULTURE AND FISHING

I. AGRICULTURE

Agriculture is the most widespread occupation in Ghana. It occupies over 70 per cent of the entire working population, while of the remainder only a very small proportion in the large urban centres are so completely divorced from the land as not to own even a small kitchen garden. The proportion of the working population engaged in agriculture is highest in the Northern and Upper Regions, where it is almost certainly over 80 per cent. Next, in order, come the Brong-Ahafo, the Volta Region, Ashanti, the Eastern Region and the Western and Central Regions.[1]

Apart from the large number of people engaged in it, agriculture is important on account of the contribution it makes to the country's revenue. Cocoa is easily the leading export of Ghana and in 1962 yielded £67 million out of a total revenue of £112 million. If the value of all the foodstuffs—worth about £180 million in 1962[2]—and other commodities grown purely for local consumption is added, it becomes quite obvious what a great contribution agriculture makes to the national economy.

A great variety of crops is produced, and important differences may be noticed from one part of the country to another. Such differences are due largely to differences in climate and soil, and the following three broad agricultural divisions can therefore be distinguished (Fig. 16): (*a*) the forest zone, (*b*) the coastal savannas, and (*c*) the northern savannas.

(a) The forest zone

This zone extends over the greater part of the Eastern, Central and Western Regions and the southern part of Ashanti and Brong-

---

[1] See 1960 Ghana Census Report (Government Printer, Accra).
[2] Ghana Seven Year Development Plan 1963/64 to 1969/70, Accra, 1964.

Ahafo and parts of the Volta Region. The chief crop is cocoa, which is grown wherever conditions are suitable (Plates 4 and 5). The largest concentration of cocoa farms today is found in the western and eastern parts of the two southern Regions and particularly in the central part of Ashanti. Thirty years ago, however, it was in the Eastern Region that most of the cocoa farms were situated. Today most of these early farms have lost all their cocoa owing to soil exhaustion and disease, especially the swollen shoot, and much of the land is devoted mainly to the cultivation of foodstuffs.

Even in the cocoa areas other crops are grown for local consumption, such as yams, plantains, bananas, cocoyams, cassava, maize, rice, peppers, garden eggs, okros, onions, tomatoes, and various fruits like avocado pears, oranges and pineapples.

The cocoa tree takes from five to seven years to mature and bear fruit, but thereafter continues to yield for several years. Cocoa farming thus gives rise to a fixed type of farming in contrast with food farming which is based on a system of shifting cultivation or bush fallowing. Under this system a plot of land is farmed for two or three years and then allowed to return to bush for a period ranging from two to ten years, depending on the amount of land available, after which it is cultivated again. In the cocoa-growing areas it is usual for the food farms to rotate around the cocoa farms or to be located within a mile or so of the larger centres, while the cocoa farms occupy the more favourable land beyond up to a distance of three miles.[1]

Shifting cultivation is a simple method of enabling the soil to regain its fertility gradually by natural means. This is done largely through the supply of humus from the bush which is allowed to grow on the abandoned farm. Where land is plentiful and the resting period is long, shifting cultivation is quite a satisfactory method of farming, but where the pressure of population is great and the period of fallow correspondingly short the soil is unable

[1] See R. W. Steel, 'Ashanti Survey, 1945–6: an Experiment in Social Research', *Geographical Journal*, vol. cx (1947), pp. 151–60. See also E. A. Boateng, 'Recent Changes in Settlement in South-East Gold Coast', Institute of British Geographers, *Transactions and Papers* (1955), pp. 157–69.

Fig. 16

65

to recover its goodness, and progressive deterioration takes place.

Until about sixty years ago farming in the forest zone was mainly on a subsistence basis. The only export items were palm oil and rubber, which were collected from wild trees growing in the forest. Cocoa was introduced as a commercial crop by Tetteh Quashie in 1879 from the Spanish island of Fernando Po. It appears that as far back as 1815 or even earlier the Dutch had attempted to grow it. But their efforts, like those of the Basel missionaries in 1857 and 1861, were unsuccessful.[1]

By 1905 the cultivation of cocoa had come to dominate all other agricultural activities in the country. The first area to grow the crop on a large scale was Akwapim, where Tetteh Quashie had actually planted his seedlings. From there it spread westward and northward to Akim, Ashanti and Brong-Ahafo. Today, some $4\frac{1}{2}$ million acres of land are under cocoa.

Cocoa is usually grown on small farms of from one to two acres, but very much larger farms are found. Planting is done at the beginning of May just after the initial burst of the rainy season. During the first five or seven years when the trees are maturing they are usually interplanted with plantains, cocoyams, vegetables and other food crops, thus enabling the farmer to derive some benefit from the land before the cocoa trees start yielding. After the first cocoa crop has been harvested the food crops are confined to the land around the edges of the cocoa farms.

Once established, cocoa farms do not need much attention beyond an occasional clearing of undergrowth beneath the trees. The main task is harvesting, which is done twice a year. Between April and July there is a small harvesting season, but the main season, responsible for about 95 per cent of the annual crop, lasts from October to February and is followed by a period of drought during which the beans are conveniently dried.

Cocoa requires a rich, well-drained soil and a rainfall of between 45 and 75 in. per annum. Excessive moisture encourages disease and causes a reduction in soil fertility through leaching. Therefore even in areas having the desired amount of rainfall the plant

[1] A. W. Cardinall, *The Gold Coast* (1931).

prefers gently undulating land with a good underground drainage. Another important requirement is the humid atmosphere found in the high forest. As soon as the vegetation is reduced to low secondary forest and bush, as has happened in the older cocoa lands in the Eastern Region, the cocoa plants begin to die off. The leading cocoa-producing region is Ashanti, followed in order by the Eastern Region, Brong-Ahafo, the Central Region, the Volta Region and the Western Region. Cocoa production within these Regions in 1961–62 is shown in Table 5.

Region	Tons produced	Percentage of national output
Eastern	81,000	19·9
Central	61,000	15·0
Western	21,000	5·1
Ashanti	147,000	36·0
Brong-Ahafo	69,000	16·9
Volta	29,000	7·1
Total	408,000	100·0

Table 5. *Cocoa production by regions in 1961–62*
(Based on *Economic Survey*, 1962, Accra.)

Although almost all the food crops of the forest zone can be grown in areas of low, secondary forest, some of them, like plantains, cocoyams, bananas and certain varieties of yam, prefer the more humid conditions of the high forest proper.

Except for cocoa and rice, which are generally grown on farms by themselves, agriculture in the forest zone is characterized by mixed cropping. Several crops reaching maturity at different times are grown on the same plot. As most of the crops are annuals, farms must be prepared afresh every year. The clearing and burning of bush takes place in January and February. On old farms this involves light work, but on a new site it may be necessary to fell several large trees. No attempt is made to clean or stump the land thoroughly before burning, and the farm has an untidy appearance. This, however, has the advantage of checking erosion during the torrential rains which follow the dry season.

Sowing begins early in April. Maize is planted first to ensure a full growing period and maturity before August. Plantains, vegetables and cocoyams are harvested between September and December. Cassava is usually not harvested until the following February, and indeed is sometimes left standing for another year.

Different crops show a noticeable preference for different types of soil. Plantains, bananas and cocoyams thrive best in forest loams rich in humus. Maize, yams, cocoyams and vegetables prefer moderately rich and well-drained loams. Cassava is the least selective, and is grown everywhere except in markedly swampy soil, and this, combined with its very high yields, makes it the ideal 'poor man's crop'.

The type of rice commonly grown in the forest zone is the swamp variety. Formerly most of it was grown in the Western Region, particularly in the Axim area, but now considerable amounts are found in Brong-Ahafo and in the Volta and Northern Regions. Rice demands careful stumping and tilling of the land before planting. The seed is sown broadcast at the beginning of the rains in April and the farm surrounded with a compact fence of stakes driven well into the ground to protect the crop from the attacks of ground rats. Harvesting takes place in August, but the period immediately preceding, when the rice is ripening, is an extremely busy one for the farmer, who must keep off crows and other birds, and the farms are dotted with scarecrows and little sheds from which watch is kept.

There are thus really two types of agriculture in the forest zone. There is the fixed type of farming to which cocoa gives rise, and also the shifting agriculture associated with food crops.

Scattered in the forest zone are a large number of settlements of varying sizes where the farming population live. The owners of cocoa estates do not always farm the land themselves, but depend on hired labour. Every large cocoa estate has its own small hamlet where the labourers live. After the cocoa beans have been harvested, fermented and dried, they are sent from these hamlets to the larger settlements for sale to the agents of the marketing board (Fig. 17a). The large and ready profits yielded by cocoa have brought about the phenomenon of the absentee landlord, who visits his estates only periodically and entrusts the actual running

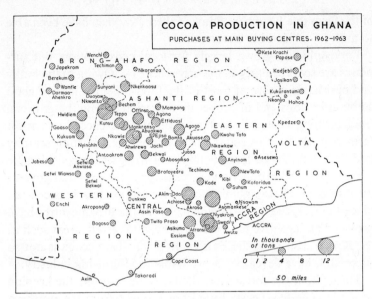

Fig. 17*a*

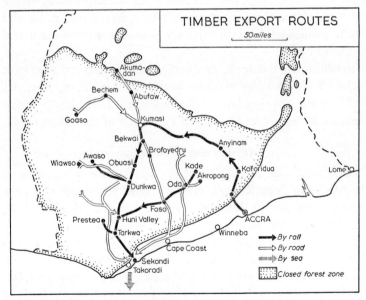

Fig. 17*b*

of the farm to a headman. Some of these headmen have been able to amass considerable fortunes.

Foodstuffs are grown largely for local consumption, but surpluses are sent regularly to the urban centres. Owing to the bulky and perishable nature of most of the foodstuffs, the lack of good communications and of proper organization among the growers, food farming is usually not as profitable as cocoa, and most farmers prefer to grow cocoa wherever possible. Wartime scarcity and the need to feed large numbers of troops gave considerable stimulus to food production between 1939 and 1946 and government bulk-purchase organizations were set up at various centres. Since the war, the increasing demands of the urban centres have provided an incentive for food farming, and certain areas such as the Krobo district of the Eastern Region, where cocoa is not so successful, have developed a profitable food-growing industry.

Throughout the forest zone the tsetse fly prevents the keeping of cattle. The few beasts found are brought from the northern savannas and are kept only for short periods before slaughtering for beef. Almost every village, however, has sheep, goats and poultry, which are kept on a free-range basis and provide a useful source of meat.

In addition to livestock, most settlements in the forest zone have various fruit trees like avocado pears, oranges, limes, pawpaws and bananas growing around the buildings. In the larger settlements such trees are confined to the outskirts of the built-up area.

(b) The coastal savannas

Broadly speaking, this region comprises the area lying south of the Akwapim-Togo Ranges. The three chief occupations here are fishing in the sea, in the coastal lagoons and in the Volta river, farming and stock raising.

Forming an irregular zone along the coast are coconut plantations. They are thickest around settlements where the land is fairly low-lying. The nuts are consumed locally for the most part, but in some places, especially in the Keta area, they form the basis of an export industry in copra.

Immediately behind the shore is a zone of agricultural land. Its value varies according to the soil, but there is a tendency for the fertility of the land to increase with rainfall from the coast inland. It is also within this zone that stock raising takes place. The topography of the coastal savannas east of Accra is marked by a succession of ridges and spoon-shaped valleys. It is usually the ridges and slopes that are cultivated owing to the better drainage of the soils there.

With the exception of the coconut plantations, which give rise to a fixed type of farming like cocoa in the forest zone, agriculture throughout the coastal savannas is of the shifting type. The end of the dry Harmattan season is followed by the firing of the grass and bush as a prelude to the preparation of the land for sowing. The most widespread crop is cassava. In the drier areas it is intercropped with okros, pepper, tomatoes and garden eggs, whilst further inland it is intercropped with maize as well. Sometimes, however, each of these crops is grown separately on individual plots.

Farms are generally small—one to two acres or even less—and they are usually located near motor roads to enable the crop to be despatched easily to buying centres. In the eastern part of the plains, where the savanna is more open, the emphasis is on livestock rather than crop production, and farms do not become a prominent feature of the landscape until the moister lands at the mouth of the Volta are reached. In the eastern part of the Volta Delta, between Keta and Anloga, shallots (a type of small onion) are grown on a large scale with the aid of droppings from bats and fish waste. Sheep, goats, pigs and poultry are also kept throughout the plains for local consumption, but the really important livestock are cattle, which can be kept on a large scale owing to the comparative absence of the tsetse fly (Plate 6 a).

The two chief factors governing the distribution of cattle are drinking water and pasture grasses. Neither the spiky, succulent grasses of the immediate coastal fringe nor the reeds and other characteristic plants of the marshy valleys are suitable for cattle. They thrive best on the Guinea grass, which forms excellent pasture when it sprouts afresh at the onset of the March rains after burning. Such pastures are most extensive between Accra and the Shai Hills, approximately south of Dodowa (Fig. 32).

There are two specially favoured areas within this zone for livestock. The first is the plains immediately east of Achimota, where piped water is able to supplement the unreliable supply from seasonal streams and wells. The second area lies between Tema and Dodowa. Although a little milk is produced and sold locally, the cattle are chiefly reared for their meat.

Despite the large number of cattle in the coastal savannas, there is hardly any attempt at mixed farming. Crop farming is generally undertaken by the local people, while animal rearing is in the hands of herdsmen from the Northern Region, and the two activities are quite separate.

Considerable quantities of vegetables are grown in the coastal savannas for local consumption. On the outskirts of Accra are a growing number of market gardens in the proper sense of the term, which supply the city with such fresh vegetables as lettuces, cucumbers, carrots, etc. The gardens usually consist of tiny plots managed on a part-time basis by people living on the outskirts of the city, especially along the Accra–Dodowa road.

The agriculture of the coastal savanna region merges gradually into that of the forest to the north, and at the foot of the Akwapim-Togo Ranges is a narrow zone combining the features of both regions. Palm trees, which are typical of the forest region, begin to appear, and ant-hills, so noticeable in the drier parts of the coastal savanna, are few and far between. Conditions, however, are still too dry for cocoa, and the typical forest crops, like plantains, bananas and cocoyams, can grow only in specially favoured spots.

(c) The northern savannas

Although the vegetation of the northern savannas resembles that of the coastal area more closely than any other region, there are important differences in the environmental conditions of the two areas. While, along the coast, there are two rainy seasons separated by two dry ones, in the northern savannas the year is divided

72

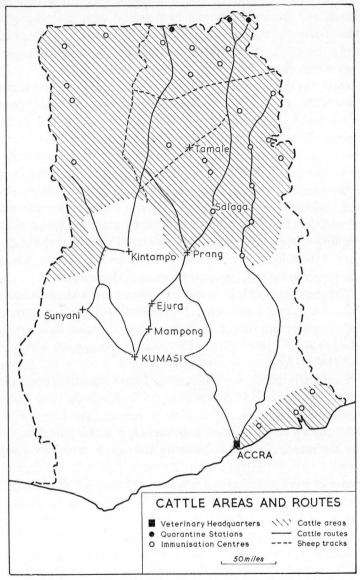

Fig. 18. NOTE: Most of the cattle markets (marked with a cross)
lie outside the cattle areas.

73

into only two seasons—a long rainy season occuring between March and October, followed by a period of intense drought. Also, compared with an annual rainfall of only about 30–40 in. along the coast, the northern savannas have a total averaging between 40 and 50 in.

Owing to the length and intensity of the dry season, cocoa and most of the typical food crops of the high forest zone cannot grow in the north, and agriculture is almost entirely confined to the rearing of livestock and the cultivation of grains and other annual crops which can mature before the dry season or else are unaffected by it. The usual crops are peppers, tomatoes, okros, garden eggs, sweet potatoes, cotton, guinea corn, millets, pulses, maize, rice and various legumes such as groundnuts and bambarra beans. In addition to these, yams and cassava are very widespread. Planting of farm crops usually takes place in April, at the beginning of the rains, and except for a few crops like cassava, which stay longer in the soil, harvesting is done in December.

The rearing of cattle is far more important and widespread here than in the coastal savannas. Especially favourable for cattle is the drier, northern part of the region, where the tsetse fly is almost wholly absent. Other animals kept include sheep, goats, chickens and Guinea fowl.

Farming is mainly for subsistence. Farms are small, and as in the southern part of Ghana shifting cultivation is the rule. But it is shifting cultivation with a slight difference. As many of the cultivators themselves rear cattle, there is a growing tendency to use the manure of the animals on the farms, especially those situated near settlements. In a few places cultivation is done by means of hand ploughs drawn by oxen (Plate 6b). This practice is most common in the area north of Tamale, where settlements consist of isolated farmsteads or 'compounds', each containing a family unit and set amid its own fields.

Although agriculture in the northern savannas is primarily concerned with the production of food for local consumption, there is a notable export of livestock, poultry and yams to other regions. Another widespread export is shea butter, which is

74

obtained from the fruit of the shea tree to be found growing wild all over the region. Yams for export come mainly from the southern section, while cattle, sheep, goats and poultry come from the northern section, which adjoins the rich livestock-producing region of Upper Volta.

On the whole, agriculture in the northern savannas is far more precarious than elsewhere in Ghana. The rainfall shows wide variations from year to year, both as regards the amount and the time when it occurs, and the dry season is so intense that unless it has been preceded by a good harvest acute food shortages may result. Hence the name 'hungry season' given to this time of the year. Sometimes the rains of the wet season may be so poor that harvests are meagre and real famine conditions may threaten.

In addition to the problems arising from the nature of the environment, farmers in the northern savannas are faced with the difficulty of selling their products readily, owing to the vast distances which separate them from the large consuming centres in the south of the country. Although cattle, yams and shea butter form a useful source of cash, they bring in far less revenue than cocoa in the forest region, and the general standard of living of farmers in the north is low, despite the fact that they are hard and efficient workers. Hence many people emigrate south as labourers in search of better opportunities.

However, agriculture here has considerable future possibilities. Since 1949 an experiment in mechanized farming has been undertaken at Damongo in the Gonja district. If it succeeds, it will do much to stimulate agriculture in this very poor and comparatively backward region.

The kind of stimulus which government guidance of this sort can give is well shown in the livestock industry, where the establishment of veterinary stations and centres (Fig. 18) has already done a lot to eradicate disease and improve stocks all over the region. The cattle industry will make even more progress and agriculture generally will benefit greatly when transport facilities to Ashanti and the coast are improved. If the Volta aluminium

75

project proceeds in the form at present envisaged, the vast lake behind the Akosombo dam will provide a relatively cheap and convenient line of communication between the Northern Region and the southern part of Ghana. At present, cattle intended for sale in Ashanti and the coastal areas frequently have to make the long journey on foot along roads and through the bush (Fig. 18). Many of the animals die of disease or exhaustion before reaching their destinations, and those that survive arrive in a poor and emaciated condition.

2. PROBLEMS OF AGRICULTURE

Although agriculture plays an extremely vital role in the economic life of Ghana, it faces several problems which must be tackled before it can make its fullest contribution to the national life.

The first problem is the question of water supply and soil conservation. Owing to the seasonal character of the rainfall in most places, there is usually a shortage of water during the dry season. This is particularly serious in the north, but in the coastal savannas, too, more crops could be grown and better pastures provided for livestock if the rainfall were supplemented with irrigation.

Farmers throughout the country are constantly faced with the threat of soil erosion on account of the torrential character of the rainfall. Again, it is in the north, where the rainy season follows a long period of intense drought, that this is most serious. The most effective way of preventing soil erosion is by keeping the soil constantly covered with crops and vegetation. This is one of the advantages of the widely practised system of shifting cultivation, for even when the farms are not under crops they are covered with a fallow consisting of bush.

The farms themselves usually have an overgrown appearance owing to the large variety of crops grown and the fact that trees and bushes are frequently left standing among the crops. If they had the tidy appearance common in mid-latitudes, the torrential downpours would easily erode the soil. Even under shifting cultivation, farms situated on steep slopes frequently suffer from sheet and gully erosion. Sheet erosion involves the progressive

76

removal of thin films of the valuable surface soil, while gully erosion leads to the formation of deep gullies across the face of the land along which vast quantities of soil are carried by torrents resulting from rains. Where the vegetation cover is very thin, sheet erosion may be considerably aided by the action of wind.

Despite its advantages, shifting cultivation has a number of drawbacks, the most serious of which is that it can only succeed where there is an abundance of land so that abandoned farms can be left under bush fallow for seven or more years. This means in effect that perhaps only about one-eighth of the land is under crops at any one time. Increasing pressure of population leads to a drastic reduction in the period of fallow, and the question which now faces agriculture is whether some other means of restoring the fertility of the soil can be found.

In countries where livestock, particularly cattle, can be kept the answer is to use farmyard manure to replenish the soil. Owing to the prevalence of the tsetse fly in Ghana, this method cannot be employed except in the northern and, to a less extent, in the coastal savannas, where the danger of tsetse is not so great. Another solution would be to use artificial manures or fertilizers, but this cannot be widely adopted because it is expensive and beyond the means of the average farmer. As an alternative, it has been suggested that the answer for the farmer in the forest zone, where cattle cannot be kept, might be to retain shifting cultivation on account of its many advantages, but to shorten the period of fallow by allowing only specially selected plants capable of enriching the soil quickly to grow on abandoned farms. In this way more land would be made available for cultivation. But it still needs to be discovered which plants would make the best fallow.

The lack of adequate transport facilities between farms and consuming centres is yet another problem facing agriculture. Many areas of good farm land, especially in Ashanti and the Western Region, are undeveloped because they lie too far from roads or railways. If people have to travel a distance of more than six miles by foot before getting their farm products to a market or convenient point on a road or the railway, they usually refuse to take the trouble, particularly as foodstuffs tend to fetch such a small price. The result is that in many remote places valuable quantities of food are simply left to decay, or else only a small quantity is grown for strictly local consumption.

Even where crops can be marketed easily because of good communications, the farmers themselves usually have to walk three or four miles daily from their villages to their farms and a similar distance back home at the end of the day's work. This reduces efficiency. Time and energy that should be spent on the farm are spent on daily travel to and from the farm. A farmer whose village is three miles from his farm walks an average distance of 30 miles a week of five working days, involving a total of 10–15 hours.

If farmers could get to their farms and back by lorry they would arrive more fresh and fit for their day's labour, spend more time on their farms and convey a larger quantity of farm produce and firewood home than under the present system of head porterage.

Another problem facing agriculture is that of low productivity. Compared with the large number of people who work on the land, the amount of the country's agricultural produce, especially of foodstuffs, is small. This is not because farmers are lazy, but mainly because a lot of their energy is wasted by the primitive methods they still employ for clearing, planting and harvesting.

Some people think that the solution to this problem is to adopt mechanization, wholly or in part. In the northern parts of Ghana where the land is free from tsetse it is possible to use ploughs drawn by oxen for cultivating the soil, but in the forest zone of Ashanti and the southern Regions, mechanization would mean the use of tractors instead of oxen. No real beginning has as yet been made with mechanized agriculture in the forest zone, but in the northern savanna region experiments with mechanization started by the Gonja Development Company at Damongo are proving successful. In the coastal savannas similar experiments, but on a much smaller scale, have been successfully carried out at the University of Ghana's farm at Nungwa and at several other places.

Mechanization, however, has its own problems. In temperate

countries, where farming takes place in open fields and the soil does not contain hard stones and stubborn roots, mechanization can be employed readily and with fairly assured success. But most of the agriculture in Ghana, outside the savanna areas, is of the forest type and the large-scale use of mechanization would require the clearing of extensive areas. Care would have to be taken to remove all large roots and stones, which would otherwise ruin the edges of the steel ploughs. The clearing of large areas of forest and bush would immediately expose the soil to erosion during the season of torrential rains. It would also deprive the soil of the beneficial effects of the bush fallow and make it necessary for the farmer to find other means of fertilizing the soil, perhaps by the use of expensive artificial manures. Once the forest was extensively cleared, the very conditions, such as shade and moisture, which many of the crops of the forest type of agriculture require, might disappear.

All these are real difficulties. In some parts of the country it might be possible to overcome them easily, but in many others they would prove too difficult. But even where full-scale mechanization is not possible at present, there are many ways in which labour-saving devices and more modern methods could be introduced into the farming industry, thus making it more efficient and productive.

Lastly, there is the problem of organization. The present method of distributing and selling farm produce for local consumption is most unsatisfactory. The result is that while in certain places there is a glut of foodstuffs, others may be experiencing acute shortages. The work of the Cocoa Marketing Board, which has handled the sale of all cocoa since the Second World War, and of the Agricultural Produce Marketing Board and the Co-operative Marketing Association, which formerly dealt with most of the other agricultural exports, shows that with better organization farmers growing foodstuffs for local consumption could sell their produce more profitably by ensuring that it was sent to the right places, in the right quantities, at the right time.

In such ways the general efficiency of agriculture in Ghana

could be greatly improved. More of the food consumed by the people, including poultry and livestock, could be produced locally and fewer people than at present would be required for agriculture, thus releasing much-needed manpower for other industries.

3. FISHING

Fishing takes place in almost every part of Ghana, and altogether some 58,000 people are engaged in the industry. There are three forms: (*a*) sea fishing, (*b*) lagoon fishing, and (*c*) river fishing.

(*a*) Sea fishing[1]

Sea fishing is the most important form of the industry and in 1961–62 produced over 40,000 tons of fish. All the towns and villages along the coast engage in it, but the main centres are Keta, Prampram, Tema, Teshie, Labadi, Accra, Bortianor, Senya Beraku, Winneba, Anomabu, Cape Coast, Mouree, Elmina, Shama and Sekondi. Each of these places has its own fishing population, but it is quite common to see migrant Fanti and Ewe fishermen in other waters during the height of the fishing season from June to September. Some of them live in roughly constructed temporary dwellings near the shore.

The boats used in sea fishing are mostly small dug-out canoes, which are made in the forest region and finished in the fishing villages themselves. Each has a crew of from five to seven and is usually propelled by paddles, although sails are used when the wind is favourable. However, the use of outboard motors is now spreading. It is estimated that there are about 10,200 canoes employed in sea fishing at the present time, including 3000 with outboard motors.

Fishing goes on throughout the year, but the best season is from June to September, when several good eating species are caught, including the large sea bream, which is regarded as a special delicacy. The commonest fish, however, is the herring, which is landed in large quantities at this time.

[1] See F. R. Irvine, *The Fishes and Fisheries of the Gold Coast* (Crown Agents, 1947).

PLATE I. The Volta bridge at Adomi, opened in January 1957. This bridge provides a through route between southern Ghana and the Volta Region (see pp. 41 and 125).

PLATE 2*a*. A close-up view of 'secondary forest' in the high forest zone. Note the dense undergrowth and the young umbrella tree (*Musanga smithii*) with large, prominent leaves (see p. 51).

PLATE 2*b*. Typical grass and scrub vegetation in the Accra Coastal Plains. A small ant-hill can be seen in the right foreground (see p. 53).

PLATE 3*a*. A general view of the Accra Interior Plains from Legon Hill. The Akwapim-Togo ranges can be seen in the distance (see pp. 53 and 161).

PLATE 3*b*. A typical view of the vegetation of the Cape Coast-Winneba plains. In the foreground is tall Guinea grass such as is found in the Accra Coastal Plains, and in the background is dense bush (containing a palm tree and a silk cotton tree) more typical of the Accra Interior Plains (see p. 53).

PLATE 4. Cocoa trees bearing pods. The mottled character of the stems of the trees is typical (see p. 64). Notice how the pods are attached to the stems.

PLATE 5. Cocoa beans drying on mats. The beans are stirred periodically by hand to ensure uniform drying (see p. 64).

PLATE 6a. Cattle drinking in a wayside pool in the eastern section of the Accra Coastal Plains (see p. 71).

PLATE 6b. Oxen ploughing in Navrongo, Northern Region. On the left is a crop of Guinea corn (see p. 74).

PLATE 7a and b. Drawing in a seine net at Winneba. In the lower picture, the women gathered on the beach are waiting to buy fish from the fishermen. While the women are local women, the men are strangers from the Keta area who have come specially for the fishing season at the end of the year (see p. 81).

PLATE 8. Felling timber in the high forest. Note the wide buttresses at the foot of the tree and also the numerous lianes (see pp. 50 and 84).

PLATE 9a. Samreboi plywood factory, showing timber being removed from the log pond for treatment (see pp. 85 and 103).

PLATE 9b. General view of Amalgamated Banket Areas Gold Mine at Abontiakoon. In the foreground can be seen pit-props and in the middle distance (left) a modern compound for African workers and (right) waste material from the treatment plant (see p. 94).

PLATE 10. Drilling rock for blasting in an underground gold mine. Note the pit-props and the miners' safety lamps (see p. 94).

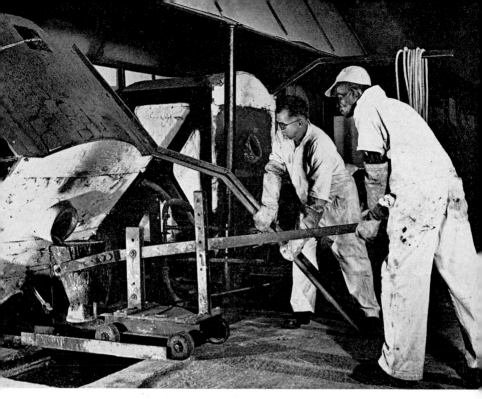

PLATE 11*a*. Pouring gold from smelter at the Amalgamated Banket Areas
Gold Mine, Abontiakoon (see p. 95).

PLATE 11*b*. Gold dredge at work, Bremang. Note the dense forest in the background
(see p. 95).

PLATE 12a. Mechanical shovel loading manganese at Nsuta. Note the 'benches' in the background (see p. 97).

PLATE 12b. The washing plant at Akwatia diamond mine (see p. 98).

PLATE 13. Oil refinery, Tema (see p. 104).

PLATE 14a. A typical compound village in the Upper Region photographed from the air. Note the intensive cultivation of the land around the compounds (see p. 120).

PLATE 14b. 'Mammy lorries' at Accra lorry park during a slack period. During busy periods vehicles stand practically bumper to bumper (see p. 125).

PLATE 15*a*. Yeji ferry on the Volta, Northern Region (see pp. 126 and 197).

PLATE 15*b*. Accra Airport (see p. 129).

PLATE 16a. The timber yard at Takoradi harbour. Note sawn timber on the quay and floating logs in the 'log pond' awaiting shipment (see p. 133).

PLATE 16b. General view of Takoradi harbour, looking seawards (see p. 133).

Various types of net are used, including cast nets, seine nets, drift nets and bottom nets, depending on the type of fish. Especially interesting is the seine net, which is cast by canoe in the shape of a crescent with the ends attached to ropes at the shore. Men and children draw the two ends together gradually until the bag in the centre reaches the shore with the catch (Plate 7a and b). Cast nets are used more often in lagoons or near the shore. For certain types of fish, hooks and lines are used.

The fishing canoes do not spend very long hours at sea. Those that go furthest usually set out late in the evening and return in the morning, but the normal practice is to set out in the middle of the morning and return in the early afternoon with the sea breeze.

(b) Lagoon fishing

Lagoon fishing takes place in most of the lagoons along the coast, and is usually practised side by side with sea fishing. It is said that in the Accra area lagoon fishing was the rule until the Fantis introduced the art of sea fishing during the latter half of the eighteenth century.[1] The species caught are generally much smaller than those obtained from the sea, the commonest type being the carp, which is caught seasonally with baskets in the muddy bottom of the lagoons after the water has been allowed to drain into the sea. Most of the other lagoon fish are caught with cast nets.

(c) River fishing

River fishing is still widespread. The rivers of Ghana are rich in various types of freshwater fish, and these are trapped or caught with hooks. Sometimes fish poisons are used to kill or stupefy the fish and so make it easier to catch them. It is a wasteful method because it tends to destroy all the fish in the area where the poison works, including a large number of small ones which are not fully mature.

Freshwater fishing is important owing to the present small catch of sea fishes and the unsatisfactory methods of distribution throughout the country. Almost every river yields some fish, but

[1] See F. R. Irvine, *op. cit.*

the most important ones are the Afram and the lower and upper reaches of the Volta. River fishing is done mostly at the beginning of the dry season. The Volta fisheries may be divided into three: fishing in the main stream, fishing in the creeks, and oyster fishing. In all, the value of fish caught in the Volta system is estimated at about £100,000 per year.

The attempt begun a few years ago to introduce trawlers and power-driven craft into Ghana and thus increase the range of fishing as well as the amount landed seems to have succeeded at last after a rather difficult start. The result has been a marked increase in the amount of fish caught, which has more than doubled during the past ten years. Thanks to the use of refrigeration, fresh fish is now readily available to large sections of the population, especially in urban areas. The prospects for the fishing industry will be further improved by the additions which are now being made to the fishing harbour at Tema. This and other moves, such as the construction of an attractive fishing harbour at Elmina, should do much to assist the development of a modern fishing industry.

4. PREPARATION AND DISTRIBUTION OF FISH

Owing to the limited facilities for cold storage, the greater part of the fish caught both in the sea and lagoons and in the rivers is cured before reaching the up-country consumer. Fresh fish is available, mainly at the places where the fish is landed and at nearby centres, but owing to the high temperatures decay sets in within a matter of hours after landing.

The most widespread method of curing is by smoking in specially built ovens to be seen in the fishing villages (Plate 19b). Fish so treated can last several weeks, and this method therefore enables places far removed from the sea to be kept supplied almost throughout the year. Another method of curing is by salting and drying. This method is used chiefly for small fish and mud-fish caught from the lagoons. It is quite effective, although it gives the fish a very strong flavour.

Although curing enables the supply of fish to the consumer to be controlled far more satisfactorily than is the case with perishable farm products, there is no doubt that a lot of room still exists for improvement. In particular, better means of supplying more people with fresh fish, at least during the main fishing seasons, need to be found. Another problem is the actual distribution of the fish to the consuming centres. At present there is a tendency for suppliers to aim at the larger centres both inland and along the coast, with the result that there is often an excess of fish in these places while other places are suffering quite serious shortages.

Fishing is a hard occupation, but owing to the way in which the industry is organized at present the fishermen hardly get adequate returns for their labours. Between them and the consumer is a long chain of middlemen, each of whom adds to the cost of the fish to his own advantage but without benefiting the fishermen themselves very much. This tends to make fish unnecessarily expensive for the consumer, except at the height of the fishing season. The result is that large quantities of cheap imported fish are consumed in the country. In 1961, for example, the imports of tinned and smoked fish from overseas amounted to 46,000 tons at a cost of about £4·8 million. However, developments in the fishing industry seem to have had some effect, and in 1962 only 20,000 tons of fish were imported into the country, valued at £3 million.

7

PRODUCTS OF THE FOREST

The 25,000 square miles of closed forest in Ghana contain a rich variety of products for export and consumption at home. Chief among these today is timber (Plate 8). The export of timber began in 1891. In those early days the industry was severely hampered by poor transport and communications, and the most satisfactory way of conveying the timber from the forests to the coast was by floating it along the large rivers like the Pra, Ankobra and Ofin. This method was both slow and wasteful, and many logs were lost through being stranded on islands in the middle of the rivers or along their banks.

From very small beginnings the industry quickly expanded. In 1913 some 3 million cubic feet of timber valued at £366,000 were exported. The First World War occasioned a serious decline, which resulted in 1933 in the very low export figure of 240,000 cubic feet valued at only £30,000. Recovery after this was slow, and in 1940 exports amounted to only 1 million cubic feet valued at £109,000.

Since the end of the Second World War, however, the industry has made phenomenal strides. By 1951 the annual export had risen to some 10 million cubic feet valued at £5 million, and in 1962 the total of logs and sawn timber exported was 25·3 million cubic feet valued at £12·22 million.

Several species are exploited, the most popular being mahogany, odum, wawa, sapele, makoré or baku, utile, emire and kokrodua. Altogether there are over 300 timber-producing species, and although not all of them have attained commercial importance, a large number are used locally that are unknown in the export trade. Indeed, before the Second World War European and American importers showed little interest in woods besides mahogany, but the value of other woods is now being increasingly appreciated, and many more varieties are exported.

Mahogany is especially popular on account of its comparative lightness, its fine texture and graining and its attractive light brown colour. It is used widely in furniture manufacture and in the making of veneers, which consist of very thin pieces used as an exterior facing for articles made of inferior woods. It is also employed in the manufacture of plywoods, of which there is an increasing output from Ghana and, also, Nigeria. Odum, which is a heavy and durable wood, is extensively employed in constructional work and also for furniture. Wawa is perhaps the lightest in weight and colour of the commoner timbers and is used mainly as scaffolding in the local building trade and for carving and canoe making, though when exported it is employed for a wide range of purposes, including the manufacture of plywood. Unlike most Ghana timbers, which are hard, wawa is extremely soft.

It is not only the exports of timber that have increased recently; its use within the country has grown very considerably. When Achimota College was built in the 1920's, for example, most of the timber used was temperate wood imported from abroad, but in the University of Ghana at Legon, built twenty years later, all the vast quantities of timber employed were derived from local sources.

Timber is exported mostly in the form of logs, but there is an increasing proportion of sawn timber, including plywood, which is made in the United Africa Company's factory at Samreboi in the Western Region (Plate 9a). Veneers are also exported.

Although bull-dozers and heavy caterpillar tractors have greatly reduced the difficulties of exploiting timber in the high forest, transportation problems still hamper the industry, making the exploitation of the more remote areas almost impossible. After the timber has been cut and prepared for export it is sent by road or rail to Takoradi to await shipment (Fig. 17b). Sawn timber is prepared by sawmills in the forest region and along the coast. The leading sawmilling centres are Kumasi, Dunkwa, Awaso, Nkawkaw, Ateiku, Accra, Sekondi and Takoradi, but there are a number of smaller centres (Fig. 21).[1]

[1] See *Colonial Report for the Gold Coast* (1951, H.M.S.O. London), and also *Gold Coast Handbook of Trade and Commerce* (Accra, 1955).

85

Altogether there are over twenty-five commercial sawmills, in addition to those operated by the mining companies and the government. Most of the large ones are owned by British and American companies. African-owned mills are few, and the majority of Africans in the industry are concerned either with the extraction and shipment of logs or with the retailing of sawn timber. One of the largest and busiest markets for sawn timber is at Kokompe, a district of Accra, and all business there is in the hands of Africans.

Firewood is another important product of the forest. In the absence of coal or other cheap fuel, the majority of households must employ firewood or charcoal for their domestic requirements. It is estimated that in 1951 more than 140 million cubic feet of wood were consumed in this manner in the high forest and coastal zones alone, and for the whole country today the figure is in the region of 216 million cubic feet. This figure is made up of 162·4 million cubic feet employed as firewood and 53·3 million cubic feet employed as charcoal, worth respectively about £4 million and £2 million. The amount consumed today must be considerably greater than this, and the figure will continue to increase with the growth of population and improved living standards.

Electricity, kerosene (paraffin) and gas are used to a limited extent for heating and cooking, but their main use is for lighting. However, there are considerable potential reserves of water-power and their development for the production of cheap electricity could supply some of the growing domestic and industrial fuel requirements. At present even some of the gold mines still use firewood for the generation of their electricity supply, although the more common fuel employed is imported oil.

The high forest is rich in various rubber-yielding vines and trees, e.g. the Funtumia tree. Before the development of the cocoa industry rubber formed one of the staple exports of Ghana. The Second World War revived the industry somewhat, owing to the loss of the important Malayan supplies, but it quickly dwindled after the war. However, rubber remains a potential forest commodity and large plantations have been started in the Western Region.

Another commercial product yielded by the forest is kola. The tree, which is indigenous to Ghana, grows in the same conditions as cocoa. Formerly there was a considerable export of kola nuts to other West African territories, particularly Nigeria, but the industry has declined considerably and most of the nuts are sent now to the territories north of Ghana.

Besides these major products there are a number of minor ones, such as chewing sticks and bath and chewing sponges, which are yielded by the forests. As the quantities collected are never very large, the forest itself is able to replace stocks without any need for planting by man. Indeed, the palm oil and palm kernel industry itself, once an important export activity and still of great local importance, can be said to be a forest industry, because in very few cases is there deliberate planting of palms by man. In most of the forest zone the trees grow wild, and man's main contribution is to promote this growth by clearing the forest and pruning the palm trees in order to render them more productive.

The oil palm is one of our most useful trees. From its fruit are obtained pericarp and kernel oil, while the stem yields a popular and potent drink known as palm wine, from which an even more potent gin, locally called *akpeteshi*, can be distilled. The leaves and branches of the tree are used for a variety of purposes, including building, roofing and basket making. With the oil palm tree are associated also the raffia palm and the cane palm, both of which are found in swampy areas. As their names imply, these palms yield raffia and cane, which serve local needs and form minor export commodities.

PROBLEMS OF FOREST CONSERVATION

On account of their great value as a source of economic products as well as a means of controlling desiccation and protecting the soil against erosion, the forests of Ghana form an important national asset, which needs to be carefully looked after and preserved.

Until the creation of forest reserves by the government in the late 1920's, there was indiscriminate exploitation of the forests and a great deal of unnecessary destruction for the creation of farms. Even so, the rate of destruction was alarming. Between 1947 and 1957 agriculture destroyed about 600 square miles of forest annually, and today out of the 25,000 or 30,000 square miles originally forming the closed forest zone only 10,610 square miles of true forest remain. This is made up of 5850 square miles of forest reserves and only 4760 square miles of unreserved forest (Fig. 14a).

Although the need to preserve certain portions of our forests is now generally realized, the desire of farmers to open up new farms in areas under forest is a constant threat to the successful conservation of forests. This is perhaps one of the greatest problems facing the forestry authorities, and it is necessary for them to keep constant watch on the reserves in order to prevent unauthorized farming or timber extraction.

However, if the work of conservation is to be really successful in the face of expanding agriculture and pressure on the land, then it is equally necessary for afforestation to be introduced on a larger scale than at present. This will enable areas where indiscriminate destruction has gone on in the past to regain some of the many advantages to be derived from a proper cover. It will also ensure that even more wood than the vast amount at present required for firewood and charcoal is available to meet the growing needs of the population.

8

MINING AND MANUFACTURING INDUSTRIES

Considered as a source of revenue, the mining industry ranks after agriculture in importance. Gold, from which the former name of the country, 'Gold Coast', was derived, is the leading mineral and has held this position for some 500 years. Other important minerals are manganese, diamonds and bauxite. In addition there are several others, such as iron, chromite, asbestos, petroleum, tin, limestone, salt, etc., which have been identified in various parts of the country, although with the exception of salt from the sea and lagoons none of them has so far been properly worked (Fig. 19). Recently, however, investigations have been going on in the Axim area of the Western Region and elsewhere for the possible development of petroleum, and excellent sand for the manufacture of glass has been discovered near Aboso.

I. THE DEVELOPMENT OF MODERN MINING

The early history of mining in Ghana is concerned entirely with gold, which was first bought by Portuguese traders as far back as 1471.[1] Most of the early supplies were of the alluvial type, obtained by washing the sands from the beds or banks of rivers, such as the Ankobra and the Birim, flowing over gold-bearing rocks.

Modern mining dates from 1877, when a French trader, Pierre Bonnat, who had previously been a prisoner in the hands of the Ashantis and knew the country well, formed a small company and began prospecting for gold at Awudua (now 'Old Awudua') on the Ankobra river below Prestea (Fig. 20). Soon afterwards he moved to Tarkwa[2], where he found already in existence a

---

[1] 'A Bibliography of Gold Coast Geology, Mining and Archaeology', by W. T. James, *Gold Coast Geological Survey Bulletin No. 9* (1937).

[2] *To the Gold Coast for Gold*, by R. F. Burton and V. L. Cameron (London, 1883).

flourishing but somewhat primitive African gold mining industry at least fifty years old.

Bonnat quickly established himself and bought out most of the African miners, and by the middle of 1882 six mining companies owned by Europeans had been established in the Tarkwa-Aboso area. However, progress was hampered by a number of difficulties, of which the chief were transport, labour and ignorance about the true nature of the gold deposits.

Transport was the first to be tackled effectively. In 1897 the government at last decided to build a railway from the port of Sekondi to Tarkwa, which meant that vital equipment and stores could now reach the mining area quickly and safely without the losses and delays encountered on the earlier route from Axim up the Ankobra by surf boat as far as Tomento and thence by road to Tarkwa (Fig. 20). The railway reached Tarkwa in 1901 and was extended in the following year to the newly opened gold mines at Obuasi. In 1912 a further railway was completed between Tarkwa and Prestea.

The labour difficulties arose mostly from the reluctance of the local people to work for the European companies, but conditions greatly improved with the introduction of labourers from the Northern Region of Ghana. Improved geological investigations from 1890 onwards also led to a more accurate knowledge of the nature of the gold deposits and eliminated a great deal of waste from mining operations.[1]

Very quickly the whole complexion of the industry began to change. The mines became better equipped and the production of gold, which had been only £32,866 in 1880, rose to £1,163,517 in 1907 and to £1,744,499 in 1914.[2]

Gold held the field alone until 1914, when manganese was discovered at Nsuta, two miles south of Tarkwa. This mineral is used in the manufacture of steel for the extraction of impurities and for making especially hard and tough steels, and its discovery at the

[1] 'The Tarkwa Mining Industry: A Retrospect', by E. A. Boateng, *Bulletin of the Gold Coast Geographical Association*, vol. 2, no. 1 (January, 1957).
[2] See *The Gold Coast Chamber of Mines, Nineteenth Annual Report*. London, 1946.

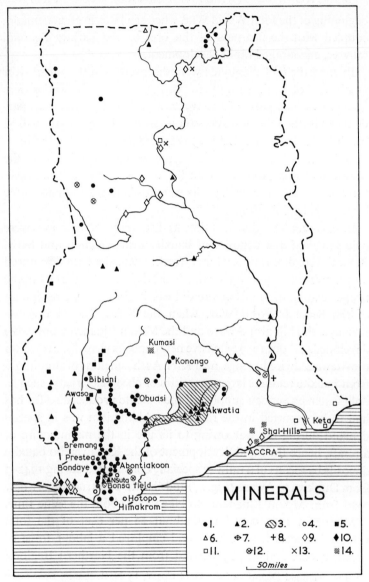

Fig. 19. 1. Gold. 2. Diamond workings. 3. Diamondiferous areas. 4. Manganese. 5. Bauxite. 6. Iron ores. 7. Cassiterite and Columbite. 8. Chromite and Asbestos. 9. Limestone and Marble. 10. Oil and Bitumen. 11. Salt. 12. Andalusite and Kyanite. 13. Barite. 14. Building stones.

beginning of the First World War, when steel was in great demand, coupled with the nearness of the ores to the Tarkwa–Sekondi railway, encouraged rapid development.

In 1919 the first diamonds were discovered on the Birim river north-west of Kibi. From then until 1924 more discoveries were made in various parts of the Western and Eastern Regions, particularly in the Oda and Akwatia areas and in the Bonsa valley, south of Tarkwa.[1] The fields at Oda and Akwatia were the most promising and early attracted European companies, but the Bonsa field was exploited from the very start by small, African prospectors because the deposits were too meagre and patchy for large-scale exploitation.

In 1921–2, about the same time as discoveries of diamonds were being made, large deposits of bauxite near Yenahin and Sefwi Bekwai were discovered.[2] Later, further deposits were discovered on the crest of Mount Ejuanema near Nkawkaw (Fig. 21), but the proper exploitation of bauxite did not begin until the beginning of the Second World War, when the Sefwi Bekwai ores on Kanaiyerebo hill near Awaso and the Mount Ejuanema ores were developed. About 1959 extensive new deposits were discovered on the Atewa–Atwiredu range, near Kibi. As the smelting of aluminium from bauxite requires large quantities of cheap electricity, such as only water-power can supply, all the bauxite produced so far has had to be exported in the raw state. Aluminium was in special demand during the war owing to its use in the manufacture of aircraft, hence the rapid development of the Kanaiyerebo bauxite deposits by means of a railway specially constructed during 1942–3 from Dunkwa to Awaso (Fig. 27) and also the construction of a new road from Mount Ejuanema to Nkawkaw about the same time.

Mining in 1962 contributed about 22 per cent of the total value of exports from Ghana and employed a labour force of about 37,000, still mostly derived from the Northern Region.[3]

[1] 'The Diamond Deposits of the Gold Coast', by N. R. Junner, *Gold Coast Geological Survey Bulletin No. 12* (1943).

[2] 'Progress in Geological and Mineral Investigations in the Gold Coast', by N. R. Junner, *Gold Coast Geological Survey Bulletin No. 16* (1946).

[3] See *Mining in the Gold Coast*, by H. G. Mountain (Tarkwa, 1938).

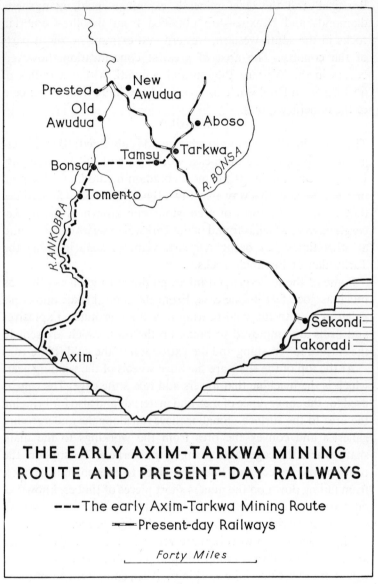

THE EARLY AXIM-TARKWA MINING
ROUTE AND PRESENT-DAY RAILWAYS

‐‐‐The early Axim-Tarkwa Mining Route
═══Present-day Railways

Forty Miles

Fig. 20

Practically all the chief minerals exploited—gold, manganese, diamonds and bauxite—are obtained from the Pre-Cambrian rocks in the south-western, western and extreme northern parts of the country. The area of greatest concentration, however, occurs in the Western Region and Ashanti, within a radius of 60 miles from Dunkwa. This area produces more than 90 per cent of the mineral exports.

2. GOLD

There are three chief ways in which gold is obtained: (i) by underground mines, (ii) by open-cast workings, and (iii) by dredging. Underground mining is the most common method, and the gold ores extracted in this way are of two types (Plate 9*b*). Sometimes they occur in the form of a conglomerate known as the *banket conglomerate*, which is found in the Tarkwaian series of rocks, and at other times they occur as quartz veins or *lodes* in either the Tarkwaian or Birrimian rocks.

Some of the underground mines go down to great depths—as much as 3000 feet in one case. From the central shaft numerous galleries lead to the gold-bearing ores underground. Explosives and drills are employed to break up the ores, which are sent to the surface for crushing and the extraction of the gold (Plate 10).

At the top of the shaft are the huge wheels of the winding gear, which is the machine that lowers and raises the cage. The cage is used for the conveyance of men and materials and also for bringing the ores to the surface. Small trolleys run along the underground galleries and convey the ores from the workings to the main shaft, where the cage takes them to the surface. To support the roofs of the galleries or line their sides to prevent bits of rock from falling down on the miners short pieces of timber, known as pit-props, are employed. As it is completely dark underground each miner carries a safety lamp to enable him to see.

The underground workings are very hot and wet. Every mine must therefore have a pump for pumping out the water, which would otherwise flood the workings. Also, cool, fresh air must be pumped continuously into the galleries and the shaft for the benefit of the workmen.

On arrival at the pit head, the ore is taken into the mills and crushed to a fine powder before being treated with chemicals, which enable the gold to be extracted (Plate 11 a). The proportion of gold to ore is very small and varies from mine to mine. In the Obuasi mine, which is said to be the world's richest large gold mine, over 1 ounce of gold is obtained from every ton of ore, but elsewhere the amount of gold per ton of ore may be only a quarter of an ounce.

Open-cast mining is much simpler and consists in digging up the ore by mechanical excavators and sending it to the mills for crushing and the extraction of the gold. This method was employed mainly at Bogoso, in an area where igneous intrusions rich in gold lie near the surface of the ground, but the field has now been abandoned. It is used to a limited extent at Abontiakoon.

In the dredging method, employed chiefly on the Ofin, Jimi and Ankobra rivers, all of which flow over gold-bearing rocks, a large dredge brings up sand from the bottom of the river (Plate 11 b). This sand is subsequently washed for the little grains of gold contained in it.

(a) Distribution of gold mines

Although there are several mining companies, gold is obtained from four major gold-fields centred at Tarkwa, Obuasi, Konongo and Bibiani.

The Tarkwa gold-field, dating from 1877, is the oldest. It covers a roughly triangular area, whose apices are at Tarkwa, Prestea and Huni Valley (Fig. 45). Several companies have operated within the field in the past, and Tamso, Tarkwa, Abontiakoon and Aboso, in the eastern part, and Prestea and Bondaye, in the western part of the triangle, have all been important mining centres. Today, only Abontiakoon, which lies next door to Tarkwa, and Prestea and Bondaye actually have mines. Tarkwa itself ceased to be an active mining town in 1956, but it still remains the administrative centre of the gold-field and the headquarters of the whole mining industry of Ghana. A little to the north of the Tarkwa 'gold triangle' is Bogoso, which until 1954, when it was finally closed down, was an important centre for open-cast mining.

Some 70 miles north of Tarkwa is the Obuasi gold-field, opened in 1897 and therefore the next oldest in the country. It is by far the largest producer of gold in Ghana, its pre-war output being nearly equal to that of all the other gold-fields put together. Obuasi, the centre of the field, has been described as 'the richest square mile in Africa'. Unlike the Tarkwa field, which has both lode and banket ores, the ores at Obuasi are mainly of the lode variety. The Konongo gold-field is also based on the exploitation of lode ores, although they are not as rich as those at Obuasi. All the mining centres on Konongo, which lies a few miles east of Kumasi. The development of this gold-field dates only from 1933.

The Bibiani gold-field, registered in 1927 but with a history going back to 1891, is the fourth. It differs from the first three in not being served directly by a railway. Bibiani, the centre, lies about 60 miles west of Kumasi and the same distance north-west of Dunkwa. It has road connections with both places, but the nearest point on the railway lies 20 miles south, at Awaso, which is the terminus of the Dunkwa–Awaso railway built in 1942–3 for the development of bauxite. The ores of the Bibiani field are also of the lode type.

Besides these four gold-fields and the Ofin and Jimi rivers, where dredging now takes place, are a number of scattered gold-fields which either produce gold now or did so formerly. One of these is the Western Akim gold-field which was centred at Ntronang and was based on the exploitation of banket ores. It was established in 1935 but ceased production in 1942. Another is the Nangodi gold-field in the Upper Region, where the Pre-Cambrian rocks emerge from underneath the Voltaian Basin. Like the Western Akim field, it had a very brief life, from 1935 to 1952.

(b) Gold production

Almost all the gold produced is exported in the form of bars, known as *bullion*. Gold has yielded a steady revenue for a very long time. At the beginning of the Second World War the value of gold produced totalled just over £6 million per annum (see Table 9, p. 137). In the favourable economic conditions of the post-war period, although the actual quantity of gold fell slightly, its value increased steadily, and by 1954 had reached £9·8 million, distributed among the existing mines as shown in Table 6. The figures for 1956, however, dropped in both amount and value, but in 1962 the output was 946,000 fine oz. valued at £11·3 million.

Gold-field	Location of centre	1954 output in fine oz. (approx.)
Tarkwa	Abontiakoon	148,000
Tarkwa	Aboso	71,000
Tarkwa	Prestea	134,000
Tarkwa	Bondaye	46,000
Bogoso	Bogoso	35,000
Obuasi	Obuasi	194,000
Konongo	Konongo	52,000
Bibiani	Bibiani	77,000
Dredging on the Ankobra	Dunkwa	32,000
	Total	789,000 fine oz.

Table 6. *Gold production in 1954*

3. MANGANESE

Although scattered deposits of manganese occur in Birrimian rocks in various parts of Ghana, such as at Hotopo and Himakrom near Takoradi, the main deposits which have been developed are those at Nsuta. The Nsuta ores occur on two parallel ridges and lie so near the surface that they are extracted by open-cast methods along benches up to a mile in length and about 20 ft. in height (Plate 12a). After the way has been prepared by blasting with dynamite, mechanical shovels strip the surface soil and load the ore into small railway trucks, which take it to the washing and grading plant. The Nsuta ores are very rich—between 50 and 55 per cent pure—and the annual production just before the war was 11 per cent of world output, making Ghana the third largest producer in the whole world.

From Nsuta the manganese is sent by rail to Takoradi harbour, where a special loading plant enables it to be put easily and quickly into ships for overseas countries. The value of manganese production has increased very considerably since the Second World War. In 1939 the annual value of exports was only

£790,000, but by 1949 it had reached a little over £4 million. From this figure there was a steady increase to £8·7 million in 1953, although production since has declined quite considerably (see Table 9, p. 137).

4. DIAMONDS

The diamonds produced in Ghana are mostly of the industrial type. The larger gem type are very rare. There are two main producing areas, the large Birim area in the Eastern Region and the smaller area south of Tarkwa in the Bonsa valley in the Western Region. The Birim field is particularly rich and the diamonds there have been worked mainly by European-owned companies using machines. The Bonsa field, on the other hand, is entirely in the hands of African prospectors, of whom there were over 3000 in 1960.

All the diamonds found are of the alluvial type, occurring mostly in Birrimian rocks. The method employed by the European mining companies consists first in the removal of the vegetation, followed by the removal of the topsoil, thus exposing the diamond-bearing gravel. This gravel is removed by picks and shovels and taken to the treatment plant, where it is washed, screened and sorted (Plate 12b). After an area has been worked out the top-soil is replaced and the ground levelled.

The method employed by African prospectors is much simpler and less efficient. Small, scattered pits are sunk into the diamond-bearing gravel, which is extracted and washed by women and children in large wooden conical calabashes. The diamonds are finally picked out by hand from the residue or concentrate left in the calabashes. The haphazard siting of the pits results in a wastage of from 20 to 30 per cent of the available diamonds, while stagnant pools collect in the improperly filled pits, thus rendering the land virtually useless for agriculture.

In 1962 4506 Africans and 120 Europeans were engaged by the mining companies, while there were some 5250 Africans in the local diamond industry controlled by prospectors, a large proportion of whom were Nigerians.

The mining companies export their diamonds direct to the

United Kingdom. Diamonds won by Africans are either exported through the banks for sale in the London diamond market or else sold to established diamond-dealing firms through the government diamond market at Accra and exported by these firms from Ghana. Diamond production has made rapid progress since the Second World War. In 1939 the value of exports was £464,000. Ten years later the figure was £1·5 million and £6·4 million in 1951. In 1954 the value of diamond exports was markedly less—just over £4 million, roughly shared between European companies and African prospectors. By 1962, however, it was worth £7.4 million.

5. BAUXITE

Bauxite occurs fairly widely in Ghana, but the largest deposits are found at Kanaiyerebo, Yenahin, Ejuanema and Kibi (Fig. 22).

Although some bauxite is at present produced at Kanaiyerebo, near Awaso, it is not expected that the large reserves which the country has will be fully exploited until the Volta Project comes into being (see under 'Manufacturing Industries', p. 101).

The production of bauxite in 1962 amounted to just over 239,000 tons, valued at about £675,000. All of it came from Kanaiyerebo and was exported in the raw state, although during the war additional supplies were obtained from Mount Ejuanema near Nkawkaw. Like those at Yenahin, Ejuanema and Kibi, the Kanaiyerebo deposits occur on the flat top of a hill. The extraction of the ore is similar to that of manganese. After the cutting of benches in the hill by means of mechanical excavators, the ore is blasted with explosives and then loaded into lorries, which take it to the railhead at Awaso. From there it goes by train to Takoradi, where an aerial ropeway enables it to be loaded quickly into ships.

6. QUARRYING

Quarrying is a widespread industry in Ghana, but its importance is often overlooked because all its products are consumed locally.

The old, hard rocks, especially quartzite, granite and gneiss, provide excellent stone for building and other constructional purposes. As these rocks are widely distributed, almost every large town has its own quarry. The Accra area, where building is most active, has several quarries, and the construction of Tema harbour during recent years has led to the development of large-scale quarrying in the Shai hills. In hilly areas, the stones are exploited above ground level, but elsewhere they are obtained from pits, whose depth is usually determined by the height of the water-table.

Two other materials which are exploited are ironstone gravel, mostly in savanna areas, and sand from the sea-shore. Ironstone gravel provides excellent material for road surfacing, while sand is universally employed for the making of concrete. Unfortunately, the extraction of sand is not properly controlled, and several fine beaches are being consequently ruined.

No figures are available for sand production, but it is estimated that in 1962 426,000 cubic yards of stone worth at least £500,000 were extracted from some 100 quarries. This excludes the vast operations on the Volta dam at Akosombo.

7. THE FUTURE OF THE MINING INDUSTRY

So far the mining industry has made a most valuable contribution to the economy of Ghana. It is estimated that the total value of mineral production from 1880 to 1945 was approximately £120 million, of which gold alone accounted for £90 million. Between 1945 and 1954 minerals contributed at least a further £130 million. The question now is: How much longer will mining continue to make such vast contributions to the national economy?

There is no doubt that Ghana has considerable wealth in minerals, a great deal of which is still untapped. Taking a long view, however, it must be admitted that unless important discoveries of new minerals are made or further deposits of those already being exploited come to light, the mining industry cannot continue indefinitely to maintain its present position in the national economy.

Mining is what is sometimes called 'a robber type of economy'. Minerals, once removed, cannot be replaced, and consequently there is a progressive diminishing of reserves. In contrast, agriculture is an almost permanent asset, and it is possible by proper conservation of the soil and good husbandry to make the same piece of ground yield crops and animal produce for an indefinite period.

Apart from bauxite, which will leap into prominence when the Volta Project comes into being, it is not certain what new developments are likely to take place in the mining industry in the near future. There are signs, however, that difficulties lie ahead for some branches of the industry, particularly gold mining.

During the Second World War a number of gold mines were forced to cease production and were placed on a 'care and maintenance basis'. There was some recovery after the war, but several mines, such as those at Nangodi, Bogoso, Ntronang and Aboso as well as a number of smaller ones scattered in the Western Region, later had to close down owing to diminishing output and increasing costs, while the fortunes of some of the rest sank so low that it was necessary for the government to give them a subsidy of £100,000 per annum for 1956 and 1957 in order to enable them to carry on. In 1961 all the gold mines, except Obuasi and Konongo, and one of the four diamond companies were taken over by the State Mining Corporation, and in 1965, Konongo, too, was acquired, leaving only Obuasi as a private gold mining company.

8. MANUFACTURING INDUSTRIES

Large-scale manufacturing industries have been slow in developing in Ghana. This is due partly to the lack of some of the essential bases of industrialization, such as coal and oil, which supply motive power, and partly to the lack of skilled manpower and of large supplies of capital needed to finance such industries. Most of the foreign capital entering the country has been used rather for the development and extraction of raw materials like gold, manganese, diamonds, bauxite, timber and cocoa, which are sent abroad to feed the factories of the advanced industrial countries, from whom most of our own manufactured requirements are imported.

The extent to which we are dependent on the manufacturing

industries of foreign countries can be seen quite readily by looking at the things we use in our daily lives. Even in the smallest and most remote village normal life today would be practically impossible without these articles, which range from clothes and food to such expensive and elaborate items as motor-cars and trains.

There are, however, within the country's boundaries a large number of small-scale manufacturing industries—some of them with quite a long history—which meet strictly local needs, and a few larger ones which produce articles both for export and for the home market.

The small-scale industries include baking, confectionery, the processing of various foodstuffs, furniture and basket making from local materials, leather work, the production of bricks, tiles and pottery, the weaving of traditional cloths from local and imported yarns, the widespread conversion of imported textiles and fabrics into clothes, the use of locally produced gold and imported silver by local craftsmen for trinkets and ornaments and the making of simple iron implements or even guns from locally smelted iron or, more commonly today, from scrap derived from iron and steel articles originally imported from abroad.

For the most part these industries take place in very small establishments or inside household compounds. They call for very little motive power and, where necessary, their limited fuel requirements are supplied by firewood or charcoal. In the larger towns, however, where electricity is produced for lighting purposes, some of the larger and more progressive industrial establishments use electrical power for driving their machinery.

Until recently, the only large-scale industries were those concerned with the assembly and repair of locomotives and railway coaches in the Location works near Takoradi and with the saw-milling of timber (see chapter 7). In the last few years, however, there has been a stronger drive towards industrialization, and an increasing variety of industries have made their appearance or are planned for the future (Fig. 21).

One of the most notable of the recently established industries is the plywood factory owned by the United Africa Company at

Samreboi in the Western Region (Plate 9a). The town of Samreboi, situated in a rich timber-producing area, owes its rapid development entirely to the plywood factory and is perhaps the nearest equivalent of an industrial community within Ghana.

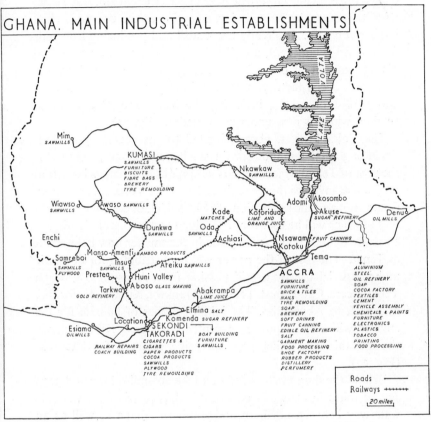

GHANA. MAIN INDUSTRIAL ESTABLISHMENTS

Mim
SAWMILLS

KUMASI
SAWMILLS
FURNITURE
BISCUITS
FIBRE BAGS
BREWERY
TYRE REMOULDING

Nkawkaw
SAWMILLS

Adomi   Akosombo

Wiawso
SAWMILLS

Awaso SAWMILLS

Kade
MATCHES

Koforidua
LIME AND
ORANGE JUICE

Akuse
SUGAR REFINERY

Denu
OIL MILLS

Enchi

Dunkwa
SAWMILLS

Oda
SAWMILLS

Achiasi

Nsawam FRUIT CANNING
Kotoku

Manso-Amenfi BAMBOO PRODUCTS

Samreboi
SAWMILLS
PLYWOOD

Insu
Prestea

Ateiku SAWMILLS

Tema

Huni Valley

ACCRA
SAWMILLS
FURNITURE
BRICK & TILES
NAILS
TYRE REMOULDING
SOAP
BREWERY
SOFT DRINKS
FRUIT CANNING
EDIBLE OIL REFINERY
SALT
GARMENT MAKING
FOOD PROCESSING
SHOE FACTORY
RUBBER PRODUCTS
DISTILLERY
PERFUMERY

ALUMINIUM
STEEL
OIL REFINERY
SOAP
COCOA FACTORY
TEXTILES
CEMENT
VEHICLE ASSEMBLY
CHEMICALS & PAINTS
FURNITURE
ELECTRONICS
PLASTICS
TOBACCO
PRINTING
FOOD PROCESSING

Tarkwa
GOLD REFINERY

Aboso GLASS MAKING

Abakrampa
LIME JUICE

Esiama
OILMILLS

Location

Elmina SALT

Komenda SUGAR REFINERY

SEKONDI
TAKORADI
CIGARETTES &
CIGARS
RAILWAY REPAIRS   PAPER PRODUCTS
COACH BUILDING   COCOA PRODUCTS
SAWMILLS
PLYWOOD
TYRE REMOULDING

BOAT BUILDING
FURNITURE
SAWMILLS

Roads ———
Railways +++++++

20 miles

Fig. 21. NOTE: A meat factory was opened at Bolgatanga in the middle of 1965 for the manufacture of corned beef.

Under the auspices of the government, several new factories engaging in such activities as oil refining and steel making (Plate 17b), edible-oil refining, nail making, match making, the manufacture of bricks and tiles, furniture making, mechanized quarrying, tyre remoulding and sawmilling are beginning to spring up in Accra,

Nsawam, Sekondi-Takoradi, Aboso, Komenda, Kumasi, Kade, Nkawkaw and other places.[1]

The greatest concentration occurs in Accra, where there are a number of small manufacturing establishments either privately owned or receiving varying degrees of government aid. But Tema, with its modern harbour, is fast emerging as the country's chief industrial centre. It already has a steel-mill producing iron rods from scrap (Plate 17b), an oil refinery (Plate 13) with an initial planned output of one million tons of petroleum products per annum, a cocoa factory, a cement factory, a large soap factory and a host of others, including the Volta Project aluminium smelter, which is now under construction (Fig. 21).

The Volta Project, now estimated to cost £G164·7 million[2] (including £G58·6 million for the smelter and £G35·7 million for the port of Tema), is far the most ambitious of Ghana's industrial projects. It involves the damming of the river Volta at Akosombo (Plate 20b) and the generation of 768,000 kW. of electricity, nearly half of which will be used for producing 135,000 tons of aluminium annually by the end of seven years in the smelter now being built at Tema. The rest of the power will be distributed for domestic and industrial use by a grid passing from Akosombo through Tema, Accra, Cape Coast, Takoradi, Dunkwa, Kumasi, Koforidua and back to Akosombo. The initial supplies of bauxite for the smelter will come from the recently discovered Kibi deposits, the Yenahin and other deposits being reserved for later use (Fig. 22).

Behind the dam at Akosombo, a lake 200 miles long and 3275 square miles in area will be formed, thus providing a valuable waterway between northern and southern Ghana as well as an important source of fish. Water from the lake will also be used for irrigation, especially in the dry Accra plains. The formation of the lake will render some 70,000 people now living in the area

[1] *Industrial Development Corporation, Report and Accounts 1955–56* (Government Printer, Accra).

[2] *The Volta River Project: Report of the Preparatory Commission*, 3 vols. (H.M.S.O. London, 1956). See also *The Volta River Project, Statement by the Government of Ghana* (Government Printer, Accra, 1961), W.P. no. 1/61.

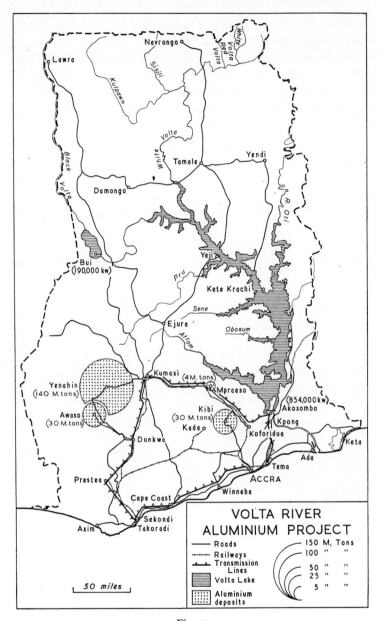

Lawra

Navrongo

Kulpawn

Sisili

Volta

White

Red

Volta

White

Black Volta

White Volta

Tamale

Yendi

Damongo

R. Oti

Bui
(190,000 kw)

Yeji

Pru

Kete Krachi

Sene

Ejura

Obosum

Afram

Kumasi

(4 M. tons)

Mpraeso

(854,000 kw)
Akosombo

Yenahin
(140 M. tons)

Kibi
(30 M. tons)

Awaso
(30 M. tons)

Kade

Kpong

Dunkwa

Koforidua

Keta

Prestea

Ada

Tema

ACCRA

Winneba

Cape Coast

Sekondi
Takoradi

Axim

**VOLTA RIVER
ALUMINIUM PROJECT**

——— Roads
·—·—· Railways
▲▲▲ Transmission
      Lines
▨ Volta Lake
⣿ Aluminium
    deposits

150 M, Tons
100 " "
50 " "
25 " "
5 " "

50 miles

Fig. 22

homeless, and steps are already in progress for resettling them in well-planned agricultural settlements.

Apart from the great contribution which the project will make to the national economy, it is of particular interest and significance because it is based essentially on the use of cheap, local hydro-electric power, which though plentiful and of great importance has not so far been exploited to make up for the serious lack of coal and other sources of power in Ghana.

The provision of cheap electricity will do much to stimulate manufacturing industries, but everything will have to be done to ensure that there are also adequate supplies of other ingredients of industrial development, such as capital and skilled manpower.

9

POPULATION AND SETTLEMENTS

Although almost all the initial capital required in the mining industry, in the building of railways and in the development of commerce has come from overseas, none of these developments or those described in agriculture, fishing, forestry and other activities could ever have taken place without the work of the inhabitants of Ghana over the years. This chapter will deal briefly with the composition of these inhabitants and the way in which they are distributed over the face of the land.

I. THE PEOPLING OF GHANA[1]

Almost all the inhabitants of Ghana belong to that stock of the human race known as SUDANESE NEGROES. These people are found throughout West Africa and form one of the five main racial groups of the African continent. Certain sections of the Sudanese Negroes, particularly those in the rain forest zone, have remained comparatively pure, racially, over several centuries, but those in the northern parts of West Africa have intermixed with *Hamitic* and *Semitic* peoples, who dwell in the Sahara and North Africa, and show this in their features. They tend to have thin lips and somewhat narrow and straight noses. Some of these mixed people are the *Fulanis*. They are generally found north of Ghana but have left their traits in certain parts of the country, especially the Northern Region, through interbreeding (Fig. 23).

It is not known exactly how long the present inhabitants have been settled in Ghana, but from the scanty records available and the oral traditions of the various peoples it appears that most of them, whatever their origin may be, have moved into the country within the last 700–1000 years.

The majority of them came from the north, but a few, such as

[1] See *A History of the Gold Coast*, by W. E. F. Ward (Methuen, London, 1948).

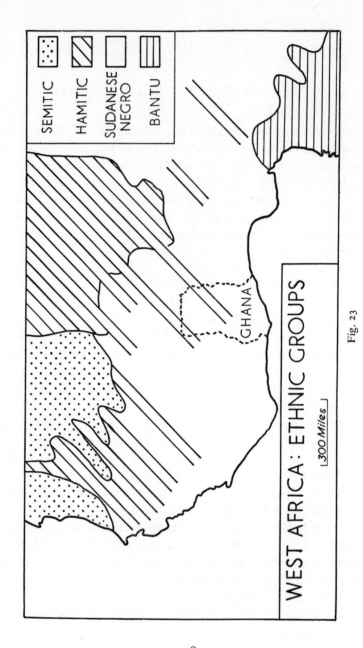

WEST AFRICA: ETHNIC GROUPS

SEMITIC
HAMITIC
SUDANESE NEGRO
BANTU

GHANA

300 Miles

Fig. 23

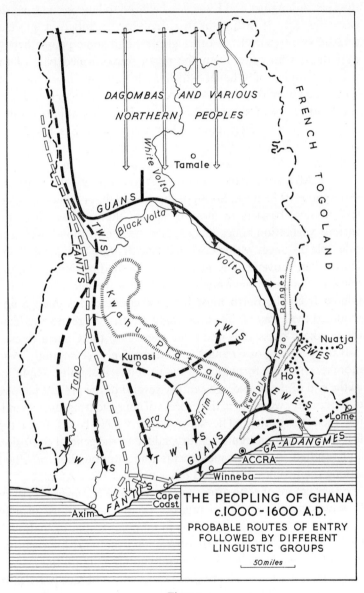

THE PEOPLING OF GHANA
c.1000-1600 A.D.
PROBABLE ROUTES OF ENTRY
FOLLOWED BY DIFFERENT
LINGUISTIC GROUPS

50 miles

Fig. 24

109

the Gas, Adangmes and Ewes, are believed to have come from the east (Fig. 24). It is thought that these movements took place as a result of pressure from other groups, and some people believe that those who came from the north once formed part of the ancient empire of Ghana, which at its zenith about the year A.D. 1000 covered an extensive area between the Niger bend and the headwaters of the Gambia river. It is this affinity—still a subject of controversy among historians—that has led to the choice of the name 'Ghana' as a substitute for the country's earlier name, 'Gold Coast', since the attainment of independence.

West Africa must have known several movements of people throughout its history. South of the great Sahara desert there are few physical barriers to movement, and the wide extent of the various vegetation zones has enabled people to move over considerable distances within environments that are familiar to them. Only when movement is in a north–south direction is there a marked change in environment, and those people who entered Ghana from the north must have experienced this change and modified their way of life accordingly, for they were moving from the northern grasslands and semi-desert into the Guinea forests.

If the peopling of Ghana is a comparatively recent affair, even more recent is the formation of the various tribal units. Right up to the end of the nineteenth century several of the present peoples of the country were still in the process of consolidating and expanding their territories. The slave trade, which lasted from the fifteenth to the nineteenth century, added to the general confusion and resulted in further movements and intermingling of blood among the peoples of this and other parts of West Africa.

Either before or soon after their arrival here our ancestors seem to have crystallized into a number of distinct groups, usually described as 'tribes', but perhaps more comparable to 'nations'. Owing to the constant threat of war and the need for security, the tribal organizations were generally along military lines.

The largest tribe of all are the Akans, who embrace practically all the people of Ashanti and the Western and Eastern Regions, apart from the Ewes and the Ga-Adangmes in the extreme south-east corner (Fig. 24). Closely associated with the Akans and forming a broad crescent on their eastern and northern flanks are the Guans. It is thought that the Guans, who arrived before the Akans, moved in along the Volta river, in whose basin they are mostly found today, entered the Accra Plains through the Volta gorge at Senchi and spread along the coast between Winneba and Cape Coast. Next came the Fantis, the vanguard of the Akans.

The Twis followed. They moved southward between the Fantis and the Guans, following various river valleys and other convenient lines of movement. They occupied almost the whole of Ashanti and spread over the forest country further south between the Tano river and the Volta. As the coastlands were already occupied by the Fantis and Guans, they stopped within some 20 miles of the sea.

Although the Ewes and Ga-Adangmes both came from the east, they arrived by slightly different routes and at different times. The Ga-Adangmes, who arrived first, are said to have come from Nigeria by a coastal route. They probably came by canoe, hugging the shore closely or travelling along the lagoons that extend from the Niger Delta to Dahomey. The Ewes claim to have migrated from a place somewhere east of the Niger to the town of Notsie or Nuatja in French Togoland, and those who eventually settled along the sea around Keta seem to have reached it from a northerly direction.

The sea has played an insignificant part in the immigration of people into Ghana. Considering the open character of the seas off our coasts, their exposure to the strong south-west winds, the dangerous surf and the lack of islands and sheltered bays affording safe anchorages, this is not surprising. Besides, with the exception of the Krus of Liberia, no West African people seems to have developed a real seafaring tradition. The surf boats commonly found along the coast can ride the dangerous surf successfully and engage in short journeys by hugging the shore closely, but they cannot brave for long the stormy waters of the open sea.

Square mile for square mile, northern Ghana contains even more tribes than the regions further south, but almost all of these are comprised within three main groups, the Dagombas of the east, the Moshis of the north and the Gonjas of the south-west. Here, too, the present tribal pattern is the result of fairly recent invasions and migrations, in which the warrior bands of the Moshis and Dagombas have played a major part.

Until about the end of the nineteenth century, when the British began to administer the 'Gold Coast' as a single unit, the various tribes formed virtually independent kingdoms, each with its own head. Some units, like Ashanti, were in process of active expansion and gaining territory at the expense of their weaker neighbours. Sometimes, as a result of internal dissension, a single state would split up into smaller units, which would in turn proceed to form alliances with other states for military protection.[1] The state which this evolutionary process had reached when it was halted by the 'pax' imposed by Britain is to be seen in the map of existing Native States today (Fig. 2).

Rarely were the boundaries between the various tribal units or states properly defined during the early phase of settlement. Usually they consisted simply of vague zones of separation following some natural feature such as a mountain chain, a river, or even a few selected trees. As populations grew and the need for land increased, competition developed for the *marcher zones* separating the tribes. In the absence of precise methods of demarcation, most of the present tribal and state boundaries have been marked by incessant disputes, many of which are still unsettled.

2. THE GROWTH AND DISTRIBUTION OF POPULATION[2]

The first population census was taken in 1891. The growth of population from then until 1960, when the last census was taken, is shown by Table 7.

It is almost certain that before the present century the rate at which the population grew was much slower than it is now. War, slavery, disease and death (particularly in infancy), were some of the factors responsible for this. The peaceful conditions which the

[1] See *Akim Kotoku* by M. J. Field (Crown Agents, 1948).
[2] See Gold Coast and Ghana Census Reports for 1891, 1901, 1911, 1921, 1931, 1948, 1960.

twentieth century has brought and the general improvement in health have contributed largely to the present rapid growth of population, which between 1931 and 1948 averaged 1·8 per cent per annum and is now (1965) about 2·6 per cent per annum.

1891	1901	1911	1921	1931	1948	1960
764,185	1,548,945	1,502,286	2,296,400	3,160,386	4,119,450	6,726,800

NOTE. The figure for 1891 does not include Ashanti and the Northern Region. Also, before 1921 'British Togoland' was not included in the census. The 1948 figure includes 6770 non-Africans, mostly British (4211) and Lebanese (1213). Of the African population 174,067 came from outside Ghana, 47,000 being Nigerians and the rest mostly French West Africans from Upper Volta. The 1960 figure includes 827,481 foreigners, mostly from other African countries.

Table 7. *Growth of population 1891–1960*

Although a growing population is a promising sign for a young, under-populated country like Ghana, mere size is not enough. If the fullest benefit is to be derived from the population, then the people must be healthy, well-educated and disciplined, united, and imbued with a sense of loyalty to their country. A small population that has all these qualities is far more effective than a large one that is unhealthy, poorly educated, ill-disciplined and disunited.

The distribution of population in Ghana in 1948 and 1960 is shown in Figs. 25a and b. The average densities for the whole country in 1948 and 1960 were respectively 44·8 and 73·0 persons per square mile, but, as the maps show, several areas exceed these figures considerably or fall well below them.

By comparing Figs. 25a and 25b one can see the changes which have occurred in population distribution between 1948 and 1960. First, almost everywhere the density has risen and there are now very few areas with densities below 10 persons per square mile. Secondly, the number of large towns has increased very considerably, especially in Ashanti. However, the main concentrations of population in the south, along the coast and around Kumasi, and in the extreme north-east and north-west corners of the country are still present, except that their areas have widened.

Broadly, high densities are found in the following places: (1) Rich agricultural areas—particularly cocoa lands—which are well served by communications for the easy movement of people

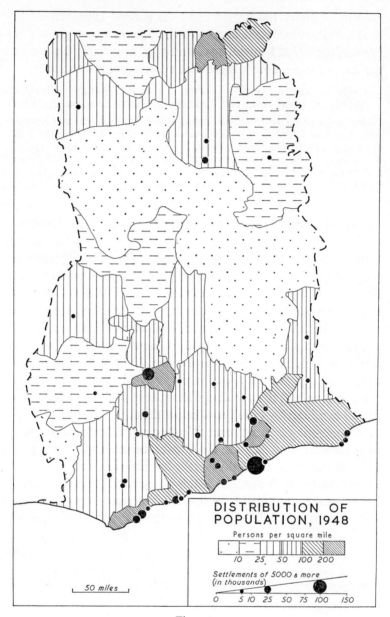

DISTRIBUTION OF
POPULATION, 1948

Persons per square mile

10 25 50 100 200

Settlements of 5000 & more
(in thousands)

0   5 10 25 50 75 100   150

50 miles

Fig. 25a

114

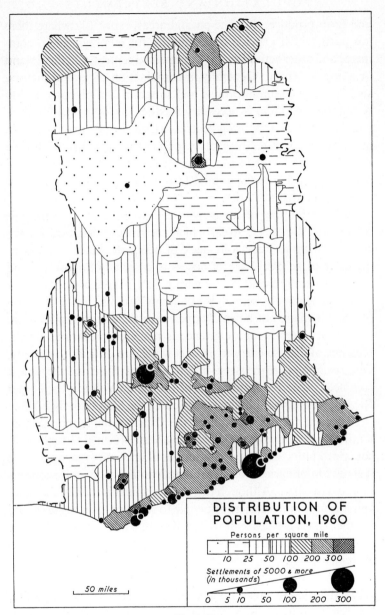

DISTRIBUTION OF
POPULATION, 1960

Persons per square mile

10   25   50   100 200 300

Settlements of 5000 & more
(in thousands)

0   5 10   50   100   200   300

50 miles

Fig. 25b

115

and farm produce. (2) The coastal areas, especially where there are ports which provide opportunities for employment in commerce and other activities. (3) Commercial centres, whether inland or along the coast. Generally, a combination of several factors, such as good communications and situation in a prosperous and well-populated area, is necessary for the development of a commercial centre. (4) Mining centres, which may or may not lie in an area that is already densely populated. (5) Administrative centres, which tend to form focusing points for large numbers of people engaged in actual administration as well as commerce and a host of related activities.

The distribution of areas with a low population density is usually as follows: (1) Areas which are virtually useless for agriculture owing to poor soils, lack of adequate water supplies or difficulty of access. Ease of access is especially important, and people generally avoid places with a very rugged topography or those inadequately served by communications. (2) Forest reserves, which are not normally open to settlement or exploitation. (3) Places where human existence is rendered precarious by the presence of disease-carrying insects which are difficult to destroy. Good examples are the tsetse-infested Afram plains and the almost completely deserted headwaters of the White Volta in the Upper Region, where river blindness caused by the Simulium fly is rife.

Historical factors also affect the distribution of population. Until very recently the various Native States formed virtually self-contained units, whose populations could not move easily outside their own boundaries in order to take advantage of economic opportunities elsewhere. Although this state of affairs is rapidly changing and it is now much easier for people to settle or even acquire land in other states besides their own, the present pattern of population distribution still bears traces of some of these earlier restrictions on movement.

3. HUMAN SETTLEMENTS

Any habitation in which human beings live, regardless of its size, is a human settlement. Some settlements consist of only a single building, while others comprise a large collection of buildings covering an extensive area and containing thousands or even millions of people.

It is usual to divide settlements into two broad types according to the occupations of their inhabitants. Those in which the greater proportion of the inhabitants are engaged in *primary* occupations, such as farming, fishing, forestry or hunting, are classified as *rural settlements* or villages, while those in which most of the working population are engaged in *secondary* occupations, that, is occupations not directly related to the 'soil' or the sea, such as manufacturing, mining, transport, teaching, office work and the provision of various services, are known as *urban settlements* or towns. Where the distinction between the two types is not clearly defined, an intermediate type known as *rural towns* may be recognized.

Apart from the work of the inhabitants, other characteristics worth noting about settlements are their actual form or appearance on the ground, how the buildings within each individual settlement are arranged and the way in which the various settlements are distributed in relation to one another. Settlements that consist of a fairly large number of buildings crowded together are described as *nucleated settlements*, while those consisting of individual or very small clusters of buildings scattered widely over the ground are described as *dispersed settlements* (Fig. 26). Not all settlements fall strictly within these two categories; some are intermediate in character. Frequently, the internal appearance of settlements and the way in which they are distributed are closely related to the activities of the inhabitants.

Settlements do not spring up of their own accord. They are established by human beings for a definite purpose, and all kinds of factors may help to determine their site and location. The site is the actual piece of ground occupied by a settlement, while the location refers to the wider regional setting. Certain sites, such as a mountain gap or pass or a river confluence, are so striking that they provide a basis for describing those settlements which take advantage of them. Thus, one may speak of a 'gap town' or a 'confluence town' or 'village', as the case may be. Even if the site itself has nothing special about it, it may enable the settlement to

discharge certain functions, such as providing a focus for communications or the site for an important bridge across a river,
which may serve to distinguish it from other settlements.

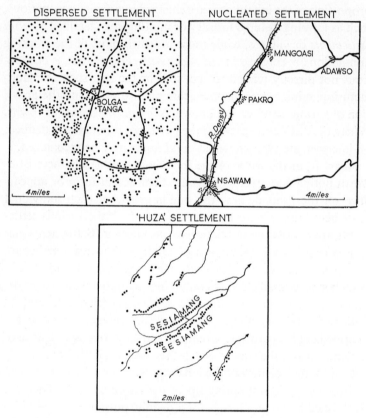

Fig. 26. Settlement types (for 'huza' settlements see p. 164).

(a) Growth and distribution

The earliest settlements built by our ancestors in Ghana on their
first arrival must have been only for temporary occupation and
have long since disappeared, either through natural decay or
through destruction by man in the unsettled conditions of those
early days.

South of the northern savannas there were three main types of settlement: the fishing villages along the coast and lagoons, the fairly large farming villages of the forest country, where large numbers of people lived together for the sake of security, and finally the very small hunters' camps in which hunters from the villages lived periodically during their hunting expeditions. It was the hunters who explored new territory and helped to extend the tribal land into empty areas. Frontier zones between different tribes came to be recognized where hunters from them met in their search for fresh hunting land.

As conditions became more settled toward the end of the nineteenth century the need for herding together in large settlements diminished, and people began to disperse in smaller settlements scattered throughout the forest.[1] The establishment of the cocoa industry speeded this process from the end of the century onwards.

The rural settlements of the three southern Regions, Ashanti and the Volta Region are built primarily to serve two purposes. They provide accommodation for the farming or fishing population and a centre for social life, in which the chief and various religious officials play a leading part. Very often the chief's house and the spot where religious rites are observed form the core of the settlement and provide a nucleus around which the houses of the inhabitants are grouped. Some villages have a *linear* plan, with the houses arranged on either side of the main routeway, while others are rectangular in shape, with the houses and their intervening lanes arranged according to a *chessboard* pattern (Fig. 44).

Originally most houses consisted of wattle and daub or of wood or entirely of swish, while plantain leaves, palm leaves or grass formed the roofing material. Today, only houses in remote villages in the forest or purely temporary structures for housing fishermen along the coast are made of such materials. Solid swish walls, swish bricks or concrete blocks and galvanized iron sheets or even asbestos and tiles for roofing are the usual building materials now

[1] See *Eighteen Years on the Gold Coast of Africa*, by B. Cruickshank (Hurst and Blackett, 1853).

found in most parts of the forest zone and the coastal region. Also the houses tend to be much larger than the simple ones of long ago.

Although the plan of rural settlements has been described above as 'chessboard', detailed examination shows that the houses are somewhat confused in their arrangement. It is only in the larger settlements, most of which have acquired urban features, that the arrangement of houses and streets shows signs of modern planning (Fig. 44). Also, in the urban settlements the buildings are more substantial and more varied as a result of the greater variety of functions discharged.

In the northern savannas, although there are now hardly any traces of early settlements, the absence of a cash crop comparable to cocoa in the south has made for a much slower pace of change. While in the forest and coastal zones nucleated settlements are the rule, in the Northern Region both nucleated and dispersed settlements are found. Also, while further south houses are normally rectangular in plan, in the north—except in the larger settlements which contain official and commercial buildings owned by Europeans or southerners—houses are generally round and built of mud thatched with grass.

The dispersed settlements of the North are found mostly in the northern, more open parts of the region. They consist of individual compounds scattered widely amid cultivated fields. It is often difficult to tell where one settlement ends and another begins. A compound is made up of a small group of huts—about five— linked together by a common wall and owned by a single family unit (Plate 14a).

Animals are penned inside the compound at night for protection against lions. The compound also contains a few conical bins made of mud in which grain is stored. In several places the compound houses have flat mud roofs, but conical roofs made of grass thatch also occur.

Owing to the large number of people from the Northern Region who are employed in Ashanti and the other Regions of the south, many of the large settlements there have developed special annexes called 'zongos', where northerners from Ghana and similar parts of

Nigeria and other West African countries live. These 'zongos' often show many of the characteristics of settlements in the Northern Region.

(b) Rural and urban settlements

Despite traditional usage, which tends to consider any settlement with an important chief as a town, only a few settlements in Ghana can be described as urban in the fullest sense of the term. The majority of settlements are rural, or at best only rural towns, although they are often spoken of as 'towns' for the sake of convenience.

Normally, the inhabitants of rural settlements derive their livelihood from their immediate surroundings, while town dwellers usually have their place of work within the confines of the settlement. As the natural resources of the immediate surroundings of rural settlements are limited, they cannot sustain a growing population indefinitely. Sooner or later, a time comes when there are more people than the land within easy reach can support, and it is necessary for the surplus population to find new avenues for employment. They can either establish a new village or else take up occupations that are not directly dependent on the land. As the number of people pursuing such secondary occupations increases in comparison with those engaged in primary ones, so the settlement begins to acquire increasingly urban features.

The size of the population in itself is not an entirely satisfactory guide for distinguishing urban from rural settlements, but it is usual for towns to have larger populations than villages. Broadly speaking, towns and rural towns in Ghana tend to be found in the group of settlements with 5000 inhabitants or more, while those with less are usually rural in character. In addition to the general distribution of population, Fig. 25 shows the distribution of settlements with a population of 5000 or more over the entire country, and thus gives a rough indication of the extent to which urban or semi-urban life is developed. Altogether these larger settlements numbered 98 in 1960 and contained a population of 1,631,200, which was about 24 per cent of the total population of the country.

10

COMMUNICATIONS AND PORTS

1. RAILWAYS AND ROAD TRANSPORT

The earliest means of transport in Ghana was head porterage. Even today it is still very widespread, and the numerous footpaths to be seen all over the country show the extent to which it is employed. Right up to the beginning of the present century, when railways and, later, motor transport first made their appearance, there was hardly any alternative to head porterage, except for the very limited use of water transport on the navigable stretches of rivers, particularly along the lower Volta and the Ankobra. The presence of the tsetse fly ruled out animal transport in all except the extreme northern part of the country and in the south-east corner, in and around Accra. Animal transport is now virtually confined to the Northern Region, where people can be seen travelling on horseback, and donkeys are employed for carrying loads.

Head porterage was both slow and expensive, and after the official abolition of slave labour in 1874 its use declined rapidly. The difficulties of the mining industry at Tarkwa during the last quarter of the nineteenth century show to what extent poor transport facilities held up economic development. The arrival of the Sekondi–Tarkwa railway in 1901 was therefore an event of great historical importance.

This railway was extended to Kumasi in 1903, and between 1905 and 1923 the eastern railway from Accra to Kumasi was completed. From Tarkwa a branch line was constructed to Prestea in the period 1908–11, and between 1923 and 1927 another branch line, the Central Province railway, was built from Huni Valley to Kade (Fig. 21). Right up to the middle of the Second World War those lines formed the main railway system of Ghana (Fig. 27).

Important as the railways were for economic development,

122

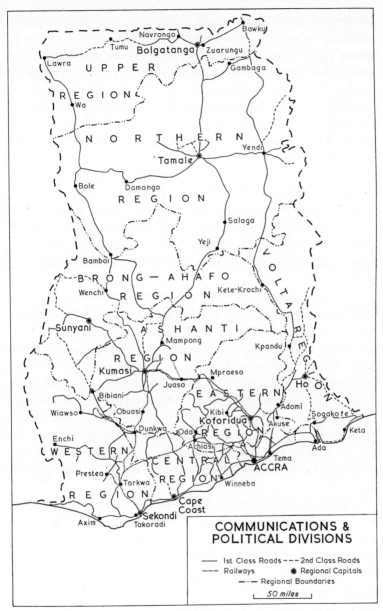

UPPER REGION

Navrongo Bawku
Tumu Bolgatanga Zuarungu
Lawra Gambaga
Wa

NORTHERN

Tamale Yendi

Bole Damongo

REGION

Salaga

Yeji

Bamboi

BRONG — AHAFO

Wenchi REGION Kete-Krachi

Sunyani ASHANTI

Mampong Kpandu

REGION Mpraeso

Kumasi Juaso

Bibiani EASTERN Ho

Wiawso Obuasi Kibi Adomi

Dunkwa Oda Koforidua Akuse Sogakofe

Enchi Achiasi REGION Keta

WESTERN CENTRAL Ada

Prestea Tarkwa REGION Tema ACCRA

REGION Winneba

Cape Coast

Axim Sekondi Takoradi

COMMUNICATIONS &
POLITICAL DIVISIONS

———— 1st Class Roads - - - 2nd Class Roads
—+—+— Railways ● Regional Capitals
—··— Regional Boundaries
50 miles

Fig. 27

123

they were of rather limited use by themselves. It required the more mobile motor-car to extend the effect of the railways to the more remote areas. Motor-cars first began to appear about 1912, but it was not until after the 1914–18 war that their use became widespread. The first heavy models were of little use, but the arrival of the light Ford with a high clearance and therefore capable of using the deeply rutted mud roads and tracks quickly enabled motor transport to become the leading mode of communication, at any rate in the south.

The combination of railways, motor transport, mining and cocoa completely transformed the economy of Ghana and started an era of great prosperity and development. With rail and road development went the construction of telegraph and telephone lines, which, like the earliest roads, first appeared around the larger towns and were gradually extended further afield to form a network.

From 1927 until the Second World War railway construction was virtually at a standstill, while roads were extended over large parts of the country. During 1942–3, however, as a result of wartime needs, a new railway was constructed from Dunkwa to Awaso to tap bauxite resources (Fig. 22), and more recently—between 1954 and 1956—the Volta Aluminium Project has led to the construction of a line from Achiasi on the Central Province railway to Kotoku on the Accra–Kumasi line, thus greatly shortening the railway route from Accra to Sekondi-Takoradi. Another line, constructed during the same period, is the one linking Achimota Junction on the Accra–Kumasi line to the new port of Tema (Fig. 21).

In spite of these developments, only a small part of Ghana is served by railways. The whole of the Northern and Upper Regions and the Volta Region as well as a considerable part of Ashanti, Brong-Ahafo and the Western Region is still entirely dependent on road transport. Even in the areas served by railways it is largely the roads that provide the vital connections with the actual points from which most economic products flow. The normal gauge of the railways is 3' 6". The majority of the locomotives formerly employed coal imported from Nigeria, but oil-burning diesel locomotives are now being introduced.

Compared with 792 miles of railways, there were in 1962 over 20,245 miles of roads, about one quarter of which are under the control of the central government and therefore kept in a state of constant repair.[1] The rest is under the Regions and the local authorities. In 1962 it was estimated that there were some 50,830 vehicles on the roads. Of this number about 25,000 were cars, including a large proportion of taxis, and some 13,000 were large passenger and goods vehicles, popularly known as 'mammy lorries' (Plate 14b).[2] The best roads are bitumen-surfaced, but the poorest ones are no more than mud tracks. In the larger towns like Accra, Kumasi and Sekondi-Takoradi large buses provide local services.

The main trunk roads are the coastal road from Accra to Sekondi-Takoradi, via Winneba and Saltpond, the Accra–Kumasi road and its continuation northwards as 'The Great North Road' to Tamale and, thirdly, the Accra–Togoland road, which offers an alternative route to Tamale, via Kete-Krachi and Yendi. Another trunk road is the Cape Coast–Bekwai–Kumasi road, which follows very much the same route as the historic route between Ashanti and Cape Coast Castle. Lastly, there is the eastward continuation of the coastal road from Accra to the border and beyond into Togoland, Dahomey and Nigeria.

These trunk roads are carried over the numerous streams and rivers which they traverse by means of bridges and culverts, but owing to the great width of the Volta no bridge existed across it until very recently, and all the roads to the Northern Region and the Volta Region had to be linked across it by means of ferries at Yeji, Bamboi, Senchi, Tefle and Kete-Krachi (Fig. 28). In January 1957, however, the first bridge across the Volta was opened at Adomi, a little north of Senchi (Plate 1). This bridge, which is 805 feet long, now carries the Accra–Ho road across the river and has replaced the ferry at Senchi.

In addition to the trunk roads are several thousand miles of

[1] *1962 Statistical Yearbook* (Government Printer, Accra), 1964.
[2] See *Gold Coast Economic Survey, 1954* and also *Colonial Report on the Gold Coast, 1951* (H.M.S.O. 1952).

second- and third-class roads forming a fairly close network in some areas (Fig. 28). Popular and widespread though road transport is, it is not without its problems. In particular the climatic conditions make road construction and maintenance difficult and expensive. Maintenance costs are very high. Even in 1954 they were over £204 per mile for tarred roads and £167 per mile for gravel roads, while the costs of re-sealing and of re-gravelling were, respectively, £1300 and £500 per mile.[1] Today, new first-class roads may cost over £20,000 per mile. However, the amount of capital required for motor transport is much smaller proportionately than that required for railway construction, and it is largely because of this and its greater flexibility that road transport has so quickly surpassed rail transport.

Formerly, one great advantage which railways had over roads was that they alone could carry really heavy loads. Now, with the increasing use of heavy road vehicles, there is hardly any commodity that cannot be transported by road, and the conveyance of timber and other heavy goods that was formerly a virtual monopoly of the railways is now done largely by road.

2. WATER TRANSPORT

In contrast with the spread of roads and railways, water transport has declined seriously. River transport, as is well known, has always been hampered by the numerous rapids that interrupt the courses of most of the rivers. However, even the navigable stretches are used for transportation only on a very limited scale. Before the arrival of railways and motor transport, the lower Volta was the most important trade artery in the south-east part of Ghana. In addition to canoes, which were employed almost everywhere along the Volta, there were shallow-draught launches plying below Akuse almost throughout the year, except from August to December, when the downward rush of flood water made navigation unsafe. Today, practically all the large-scale traffic on the river is confined to the ferries (Plate 15 a).

[1] See *Gold Coast Economic Survey, 1954*, and also *Colonial Report on the Gold Coast, 1951* (H.M.S.O. 1952).

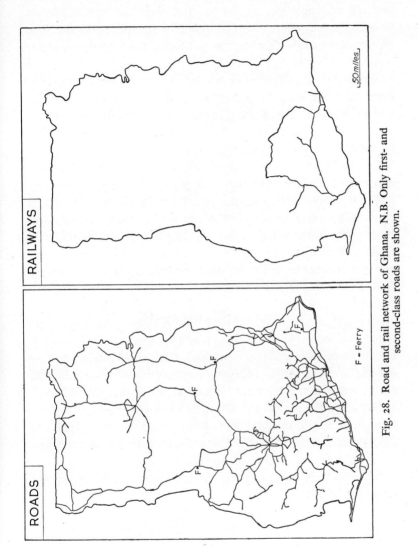

ROADS

RAILWAYS

50 miles

F = Ferry

Fig. 28. Road and rail network of Ghana. N.B. Only first- and second-class roads are shown.

127

Another important use of rivers before the establishment of road and rail transport was for the floating of timber from the forest zone to the sea, where it was collected for shipment overseas. The chief rivers used in this way were the Pra, the Ankobra and the Tano (see chapter 7).

When the Volta Project comes into being the Volta river may once again become an important waterway, on account of the lake which will form above the gigantic dam at Akosombo. Thus a cheaper alternative route will be created to the existing roads that connect the northern savannas and the coast.

As a result of the extreme southerly position of our coast and its almost straight character, the sea is practically useless as a route-way for places within Ghana. Apart from passenger and cargo boats which ply between West Africa and Europe, America and other parts of the world, there is hardly any coastwise traffic in Ghana. Periodically, fishermen from one part of the coast may move to another by canoe, but their normal practice is to operate from fixed bases on the shore.

3. AIR TRANSPORT

Before the Second World War air transport was quite insignificant, but the special strategic position which West Africa came to occupy for the Western Allies because of enemy interference with the Mediterranean and Suez routeway and the campaigns in North Africa made the region an important focus for air routes linking Europe, America, the Middle and Far East and various parts of the African continent itself. Accra airport was among the many West African airports that benefited particularly from these developments in air transport. Its runways were extended and many new additions made.

Besides Accra, Sekondi, Kumasi and Tamale have airports, all of which are now linked together by internal services. But the major airport is the one at Accra, which is used by several inter-national airlines, such as Air France, Air Liban, British Overseas Airways Corporation, British United, Ethiopian Airline, K.L.M., Nigerian Airways, Pan American World Airways, Union Aéromaritime de Transport, as well as Ghana Airways Corporation, which is also responsible for the internal services of Ghana (Fig. 29). In 1962 some 182,000 passengers used airports in Ghana.

Air transport handles mainly passengers and mail. Apart from a few valuable but non-bulky export products, such as diamonds and gold bullion, and some special imports requiring fast transport, very little cargo is handled by air (Plate 15 b).

Certain features of the West African climate, in particular the Harmattan haze, the incidence of low cloud during the rainy seasons, and violent storms associated with line squalls, present quite serious problems for air navigation. It is therefore all the more remarkable that air transport has been able to establish itself as a speedy and reasonably safe method of transport, which continues to grow in scale and popularity.

4. SEAPORTS

Nearly the whole of Ghana's overseas trade now passes through the two ports of Takoradi and Tema, which are equipped with deep-water harbours within artificially constructed breakwaters. But until 1962, a year after the opening of Tema harbour, a number of roadstead ports, namely, Accra, Cape Coast, Winneba and Keta, were in operation, with Accra ranking quite close in importance to Takoradi (Fig. 30).

Very considerable increases have taken place in the tonnage of goods handled by Ghana ports since the beginning of the Second World War. In the period 1936–39 imports averaged 469,000 tons and exports 735,000 tons per annum. During 1946–50 the annual averages for imports and exports handled by the ports rose to 665,000 tons and 1,281,000 tons respectively, while in the period 1951–55 they rose still further to 1,169,000 tons and 1,396,000 tons respectively. By 1961 the figures had reached 2,548,000 tons for exports and 1,907,000 tons for imports.[1] The

[1] For these figures and other information on ports see *The United Africa Company Limited Statistical and Economic Review*, no. 19, March 1957; *Economic Survey 1962* (Government Printer, Accra); and *Ghana's New Town and Harbour, Tema* (Ministry of Information, Accra, 1961).

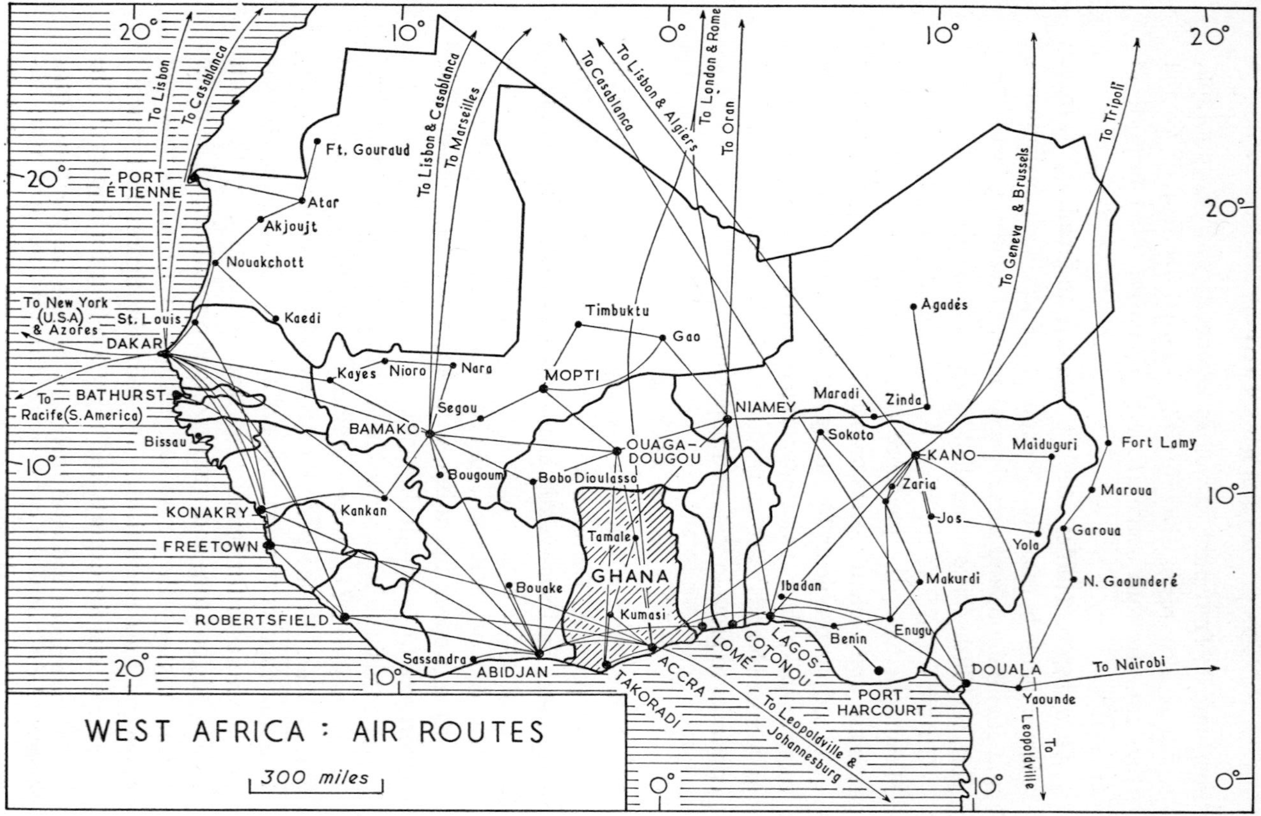
WEST AFRICA : AIR ROUTES
300 miles
To Lisbon
To Casablanca
PORT ÉTIENNE
Ft. Gouraud
Atar
Akjoujt
Nouakchott
Kaedi
To New York (U.S.A) & Azores
St. Louis
DAKAR
To Racife (S. America)
BATHURST
Bissau
KONAKRY
FREETOWN
ROBERTSFIELD
Kankan
Kayes
Nioro
Nara
Segou
BAMAKO
Bougoum
To Lisbon & Casablanca
To Marseilles
Timbuktu
Gao
MOPTI
OUAGA-DOUGOU
Bobo Dioulasso
Bouake
Sassandra
ABIDJAN
GHANA
Tamale
Kumasi
TAKORADI
ACCRA
LOMÉ
COTONOU
LAGOS
To Casablanca
To Lisbon & Algiers
To London & Rome
To Oran
NIAMEY
Maradi
Zinda
Agadès
Sokoto
KANO
Zaria
Jos
Ibadan
Benin
Enugu
Makurdi
Maiduguri
Yola
PORT HARCOURT
To Leopoldville & Johannesburg
To Geneva & Brussels
To Tripoli
Fort Lamy
Maroua
Garoua
N. Gaounderé
DOUALA
Yaounde
To Nairobi
To Leopoldville
20°
10°
0°

Fig. 29

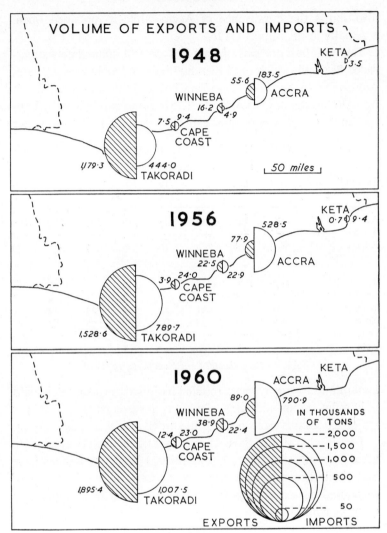

Fig. 30

result of all this has been very great congestion at the ports, particularly at Takoradi, which until the construction of Tema was the best equipped for both cargoes and passengers. Takoradi's position as the leading port is well brought out by Table 8, which also shows the importance of Accra while it remained open, especially in the import trade.

Takoradi harbour was opened in 1928 and immediately superseded Sekondi, which until then had been the main western gateway and the terminus of the railway between the coast and the rich hinterland extending to Ashanti. The harbour was originally built to handle a total import-and-export cargo of 1 million tons per

Port	1948	1950	1952	1954	1956	1958	1960	1962
IMPORTS (thousand tons)								
Takoradi	444	585	711	719	790	1397	1844	1760
Cape Coast	9	22	17	23	24	20	23	4
Winneba	5	21	12	21	23	23	22	4
Accra	184	245	312	387	528	583	791	205
Tema	—	—	—	—	—	—	—	801
Keta	3	8	4	10	9	7	—	10
EXPORTS (thousand tons)								
Takoradi	1179	1280	1316	1157	1529	1525	1895	1562
Cape Coast	7	8	7	6	4	4	12	7
Winneba	16	19	21	23	22	23	39	—
Accra	56	66	55	60	78	65	89	—
Tema	—	—	—	—	—	—	—	213
Keta	—	—	—	—	1	—	—	—

Table 8. *Cargo handled at Ghana ports, 1948–62*[1]

annum and for many years fulfilled its functions adequately with only a few minor additions. By 1951, however, it was clear that major extensions were needed and work was vigorously begun.

The original size of the area enclosed by the breakwaters—220 acres—remains the same, but additional berths and sheds have been built and several improvements made in the handling of cargo and passengers. There are now seven berths alongside the quay in addition to the moorings for eight ocean-going vessels which can be served by lighters inside the harbour. Additional wharves have been built for timber, bauxite and general cargo, as well as two-storey transit sheds and new road and rail approaches to the new installations. Both bauxite and manganese are now

[1] This table is based on figures from *Annual Report on External Trade, 1953 and 1956* (Government Printer, Accra) and from *1962 Statistical Year Book* (Government Printer, Accra).

loaded mechanically and a special 'log pond' has been constructed for the storage of logs awaiting shipment, while shed and open accommodation has been provided for sawn timber and for logs which are too heavy to float (Plate 16*a* and *b*).

Like most West African harbours, Takoradi harbour is not affected very much by tides and can therefore be entered and left quite easily by ships, without any interruptions due to great variations between high and low tide.

Although Takoradi is admirably situated for the trade of Ashanti and the Western Region, it was previously handicapped by the great length of the railway distance to Accra, which is 357 miles, as compared with 168 to Kumasi and 100 miles to Kade, the terminus of the Central Province railway. This was because until the construction of the Achiasi–Kotoku link between the Central Province line and the Accra–Kumasi line the only through rail connection between Takoradi and Accra was by way of Kumasi. The Achiasi–Kotoku link has now shortened this distance by 165 miles, but it is not likely that it will greatly increase Takoradi's hold on the trade of the Eastern Region and the Volta Region, which now have their own modern harbour at Tema.

The need for an additional modern port in Ghana besides Takoradi was felt many years ago, but the construction of Tema harbour, begun in 1954 and completed in 1960, was prompted primarily by the special needs of the Volta Aluminium Project. The main harbour encloses 430 acres of deep water between two breakwaters totalling 12,000 feet in length and contains two quays, each with four berths and ample storage facilities. There are also a fitting-out quay, a dry dock and an oil berth. Adjoining the main harbour is a fishing harbour which originally had 20 acres of water but is now in process of expansion.

A notable feature of the port are the facilities for the storage and loading of cocoa. These comprise two sheds, believed to be the biggest of their kind in the world, each measuring 170 feet by 440 feet. By means of a covered conveyor arrangement cocoa can be loaded mechanically direct into the holds of ships with little handling.

133

Since the opening of Tema harbour, the former roadstead ports at Cape Coast, Winneba, Accra and Keta have all ceased to function, and all the country's overseas trade is now handled by Takoradi and Tema. There is no doubt, however, that while they lasted, these ports served a very useful purpose in relieving congestion at Takoradi and providing easier and sometimes cheaper outlets and inlets for the trade of their respective hinterlands (see Table 8, p. 132, Figs. 32 and 35 and also Plate 17 a).

There is as yet no clear-cut separation between the functions and hinterlands of Tema and Takoradi. However, there is a tendency for Tema to serve the eastern part of the country while Takoradi serves the western part. Also, all timber exports are handled by Takoradi and all cocoa exports by Tema. As regards passenger services, mail boats bound for Europe stop at Takoradi for the embarkation of passengers, while Tema serves as the port of disembarkation on the return journey.

Although an increasing proportion of Ghana's seaborne trade is carried by the national shipping company, the Black Star Line, foreign companies serving other West African ports still handle the greater portion. Among these companies are Elder Dempster Lines Limited, Holland West Africa Line, Palm Line Limited, Delta Line, Scandinavian West Africa Line and many others from Japan, Israel, the Soviet Union and France.

Most of the vessels are cargo boats, and the only real passenger liners are the Elder Dempster mail boats, which provide a fortnightly service between West Africa and Liverpool. Some of the cargo boats also carry passengers, but even so these services are hardly adequate, and a large and growing proportion of people travelling between Ghana and Europe now go by air.

11

TRADE

I. INTERNAL TRADE

The internal trade is largely concerned with the sale of locally grown foodstuffs and a few simple manufactured articles and handicrafts. Although it usually receives far less attention than the external trade, it makes a very important contribution to the national economy. In 1962 it was estimated that the value of foodstuffs grown locally was about £180 million, and if this is added to the value of other local produce, for which no detailed figures are available, it becomes apparent that the dimensions of the internal trade are quite considerable.

With the exception of yams, of which there are large and regular exports from the Northern Region and the Krachi area of the Volta Region into other parts of Ghana, most of the foodstuffs grown are consumed within the regions where they are produced, and the buying and selling which goes on takes place almost entirely between the larger urban and semi-urban settlements and the rural areas within each region. The Central and Eastern Regions, especially the latter, are the largest producers of foodstuffs, followed by the Northern and Upper Regions, Ashanti and Brong-Ahafo, with roughly the same output.

Trade between the different regions is restricted to those products which are in wide demand but are found only in a few special areas for one reason or another. Thus, fish and salt from the coastal areas find their way into most parts of the country, while cattle from the Northern Region are sent to all the remaining areas.

[1] Most of the information in this chapter is based on: *Gold Coast Handbook of Trade and Commerce, 1955*; *Colonial Office Annual Reports on the Gold Coast* (since 1946); *Gold Coast Economic Survey, 1953, 1954, 1955*; *Annual Trade Report for the Gold Coast, 1953–6*; *Gold Coast Statistics of External Trade, 1935–53*; *Annual Report on External Trade, 1953 and 1954*; *Monthly Accounts relating to External Trade of the Gold Coast (or Ghana), 1951–63*; *1962 Statistical Year Book* (Government Printer, Accra); *Ghana Economic Survey, 1963*.

2. EXPORTS

The principal exports of Ghana are: cocoa, timber, gold, diamonds and manganese. Together with a few minor ones these exports totalled about £115 million in 1954 and £112 million in 1962 (see Tables 9 and 11). Among the minor exports the leading items are cocoa butter, kola nuts, bauxite, copra and palm kernels. Coffee, which was relatively unimportant before, has now become quite prominent, and in 1962 some 33,000 cwt. of both roasted and raw coffee were exported, worth £418,000.

Apart from the great increase in the output and value of cocoa, there have been significant increases since the Second World War in the value of almost all exports, especially diamonds, manganese and timber. Also, although it only forms one of the minor exports as yet, the presence of bauxite on the list of exports is noteworthy, since it is a phenomenon dating from the war and due entirely to wartime demands for aluminium.

The list of exports shows that Ghana is still essentially a producer of raw materials. Even more striking is the extent to which the country depends on cocoa, timber and a few minerals for its revenue. Since the Second World War the cocoa industry has been very fortunate in the high prices paid for cocoa in world markets. The result is that although the actual amount of cocoa has only about doubled, its value has increased over twelve times.

There is no guarantee, however, that this state of affairs will last indefinitely. Many people in Ghana still have vivid memories of the economic hardships which were experienced in the early 1930's when cocoa prices dropped suddenly to very low levels. Any serious decline in price today would spell even greater economic disaster in view of the extensive development projects on which the country has embarked. It is for this reason that the development of alternative exports and, more particularly, of manufacturing industries is so very important.

136

	1939	1950	1952	1954	1956	1962
(a) Principal exports						
Cocoa (tons)	280,709	267,401	212,005	214,148	234,406	421,000
	£5,101,219	£54,604,292	£52,533,085	£84,598,864	£51,062,516	£67,022,800
Gold (fine oz)	793,099	705,182	704,594	788,736	599,340	946,000
	£6,177,725	£8,718,623	£9,238,070	£9,807,462	£7,488,781	£11,253,800
Diamonds (carats)	1,087,651	1,138,102	2,133,873	2,159,224	2,518,563	3,327,000
	£464,438	£2,678,552	£5,399,885	£4,088,923	£7,920,446	£7,424,300
Manganese (tons)	336,312	711,367	794,192	460,245	635,851	476,000
	£789,606	£5,007,411	£8,722,222	£5,137,713	£7,043,796	£5,500,000
Timber logs (cu. ft.)	527,691	8,158,814	5,912,660	12,615,153	15,404,160	15,987,500*
	£54,950	£2,757,717	£2,282,170	£3,641,154	£5,165,220	£5,803,000
sawn (cu. ft.)	—	2,057,114	2,973,653	5,189,848	7,315,863	9,321,000
	—	£1,118,833	£1,823,205	£3,016,484	£4,299,724	£6,434,000
(b) Minor exports						
Bauxite (tons)	—	114,948	74,368	163,516	137,872	286,800
	—	£223,467	£137,581	£287,738	£331,207	£657,000
Copra (tons)	840	800	4,889	3,587	4,722	1,220
	£6,346	£36,070	£327,912	£284,284	£227,781	£49,000
Palm kernels (tons)	4	4,126	6,315	8,734	11,530	785
	£39	£130,835	£361,837	£515,730	£525,537	£35,000
Kola nuts (cwt.)	92,655	107,609	110,385	94,565	80,868	185,000
	£101,130	£321,393	£412,103	£272,982	£233,418	£1,428,000
Cocoa butter (tons)	—	—	5,678	795	2,726	11,600
	—	—	£1,540,287	£178,695	£550,961	£2,833,000

* Hop ft.

Table 9. *Exports: amounts and values*

3. IMPORTS

In contrast with the exports, which are mainly primary articles, the imports are mostly manufactured goods (see Table 10). The principal items are cotton piece goods, motor vehicles and spare parts, machinery and parts, oils and petroleum products and apparel. Other important items worth noting are live animals, drinks, tinned fish, rice, flour and building materials.

	1939	1950	1952	1954	1962
Live animals	254	2,125	1,558	2,018	3,043
Meat, canned and others	132	783	895	1,373	609
Fish, canned and others	182	1,015	1,778	1,946	2,977
Flour and meal	146	1,172	1,785	1,985	2,787
Rice	93	564	143	220	3,760
Sugar	118	812	1,082	1,280	2,665
Drinks (beer and stout)	85	1,057	1,539	1,354	473
Tobacco (manufactured and unmanufactured)	266	1,135	1,923	1,581	559[1]
Oils and petroleum products	555	2,572	3,944	4,158	6,057
Soap and detergents	87	659	1,006	1,234	3,112
Silk and artificial silk piece goods	98	1,357	2,544	3,960	— [2]
Cotton piece goods	974	8,596	9,577	10,051	12,475
Jute bags and sacks	125	729	1,324	289	1,757
Cement	188	1,173	1,912	1,888	2,952
Road motor vehicles and spare parts	203	2,966	4,480	4,623	4,649
Railway equipment	104	108	888	455	47
Machinery and parts	956	3,081	3,916	5,562	12,402
Clothing (apparel, including footwear)	189	.862	1,353	2,224	2,725
Medicines and drugs	102	581	996	1,016	2,080

Table 10. *Principal imports by value (£ thousands)*

[1] This figure is only for unmanufactured tobacco.
[2] Figure not available owing to adoption of different classification.

As with exports, great increases have taken place in the value of imports since the war. Just as cocoa dominates exports, so also cotton and other piece goods stand out prominently in the list of imports. But with the development of manufacturing industries in Ghana, the pattern is beginning to change.

Exports

Year	Total imports £	Total £	Domestic produce £	Foreign produce £
1939	7,541,000	13,118,000	12,841,000	277,000
1950	48,129,000	77,407,000	76,237,000	1,170,000
1951	63,793,000	91,990,000	90,001,000	1,990,000
1952	66,611,000	86,377,000	84,287,000	2,090,000
1953	73,803,000	89,943,000	87,994,000	1,949,000
1954	71,050,000	114,595,000	113,232,000	1,363,000
1955	87,877,000	95,661,000	95,159,000	503,000
1956	88,920,000	86,599,000	85,936,000	663,000
1957	96,685,000	91,602,000	90,946,000	656,000
1958	84,593,000	104,558,000	103,805,000	753,000
1959	113,024,000	113,359,000	112,753,000	606,000
1960	129,617,000	115,989,000	114,416,000	1,573,000
1961	142,830,000	115,135,000	113,174,000	1,961,000
1962	117,492,000	114,997,000	111,638,000	3,359,000

Table 11. *Total value of imports and exports for 1950 and subsequent years (figures for 1939 are given for comparison)*

NOTES

1. The total value of the country's foreign trade is obtained by adding the figures for imports and exports during each particular year.

2. The term 'Foreign produce' under 'Exports' refers to those items which come from abroad but are subsequently re-exported from Ghana.

4. DIRECTION OF TRADE

Ghana trades with well over sixty overseas countries, mostly in Europe and Africa, though in terms of value the bulk of the trade is with only a small group of countries. In 1962 the chief buyers of our exports were the United Kingdom, the United States of America, Western Germany and the Netherlands. These countries alone accounted for over 50 per cent of the export trade. Other important buyers of our exports were the U.S.S.R., Japan, Upper Volta, Canada, Norway, Belgium and Luxembourg, Sweden, Yugoslavia, Eire and Australia. The principal buyers of cocoa during the same period were the United States of America, Western Germany, the United Kingdom and the Netherlands, which took respectively 26 per cent, 18 per cent, 12·2 per cent and 12·1 per cent of the export crop. These were followed by the U.S.S.R., Italy and Japan, with imports amounting respectively to 6 per cent, 3·8 per cent and 3 per cent of the crop.

While cocoa exports were thus widely distributed, practically all exports of timber, gold, manganese, diamonds and bauxite continued to go to the United Kingdom and the United States of America, although an increasing proportion of these products began to find their way to the U.S.S.R. and other Eastern European countries which are now sending exports to Ghana.

Among the chief suppliers of imports in 1962 the United Kingdom stood first, as in previous years, followed by the United States of America, the Netherlands, Western Germany and Japan. These countries alone accounted for some 62 per cent of the country's total imports. Other significant importing countries were Upper Volta, the main supplier of livestock to Ghana, followed by India, Canada and France. It is noteworthy that the Republic of South Africa, formerly Ghana's leading customer on the African continent both for exports and for imports, ceased in 1962 to figure in the country's trade because of the decision of the Ghana government to end all trade with that country in protest against its *apartheid* policy.

PART III

REGIONAL PATTERN

12

GEOGRAPHICAL REGIONS OF GHANA

In the first two parts of this book the main elements which make up the complete geographical picture of Ghana have been considered in their various aspects. The picture is, of course, not the same everywhere. As the individual elements change in character from place to place, so also the resulting geographical picture changes from one part of the country to another.

Although such changes are frequently very gradual and the resulting variety is almost infinite, it is possible to recognize areas —some small, others large—within which certain broad physical and human similarities prevail and mark them off from other areas. Such areas are known as *geographical regions*.

As a result of its physical features and the way in which these features affect and are in turn affected by man's activities, each geographical region in the course of time develops its own special character or *personality*, which makes it stand out clearly from other regions. Although all the geographical features present are responsible for giving a geographical region its personality, it is quite common to find that in many cases a particular feature or group of features plays an outstanding part in determining this personality. This is very much like personality in human beings, which is determined by all the characteristics of an individual. And yet it is common to find in certain persons a particular characteristic or set of characteristics which seems to dominate all the rest in determining personality. In one person it may be height and build, in another it may be facial expression, or gait or voice. It is dangerous to press the analogy too far, but it is roughly in this way that differences in the personality of geographical regions come about.

The areas of geographical regions and the boundaries which divide them from each other are not fixed permanently. Just as the various elements or features which make up the geography of any particular place are changing all the time, so also the regions based on these elements are constantly changing their areas and boundaries. Some regions may even give way to completely new ones with entirely different personalities of their own. Take, for example, an agricultural region in which valuable mineral deposits are discovered. As a result of this discovery it may be transformed partly or wholly into a mining or industrial region, depending on the nature and extent of the deposits and other geographical factors. Later on, when the minerals are exhausted, a new pattern of life may come into being, thus giving the region yet a different personality.

Owing to the large number of factors that have to be taken into account and the lack of definite and universally accepted guiding principles or *criteria* for the purpose, the division of a country into geographical regions is usually difficult, and different people tend to have different ideas as to what the appropriate divisions should be. Also, some people may be content with broad divisions, while others may insist on more detailed and smaller ones. In spite of this, the division of a country into geographical regions is worth attempting, because it aids the study of its geography by providing convenient units in which are summarized the country's essential characteristics, while the very process of making such division helps to give the student an intimate understanding of the geography of the country concerned.

In this chapter an attempt is made to divide Ghana into broad geographical regions (Fig. 31). It is hoped that the student himself may in some areas be able to embark on more detailed regional subdivision based either on his own observation or on information derived from maps and existing literature.

Ghana is predominantly an agricultural country, and climate, soils and vegetation, which are the chief factors influencing agriculture throughout the country, also provide the most satisfactory basis or framework for making a division into broad geographical regions. There are three main agricultural zones: the forest, the coastal savannas and the northern savannas. By considering various factors ranging from the purely physical ones, such as

PLATE 17*a*. Surf boats loading cocoa in Accra harbour for ships anchored in the roadstead before its closure in 1962 (see pp. 4 and 129).

PLATE 17*b*. Kwame Nkrumah Steelworks, Tema (see p. 104).

PLATE 18a. Young cassava and maize growing on a roadside farm in the Accra Interior Plains (see p. 148).

PLATE 18b. Kwame Nkrumah Avenue, Accra, looking north. On the left are modern commercial buildings and on the right are part of the main market and a mixture of smaller shops and dwelling houses (see p. 152).

PLATE 19*a*. Architectural contrasts in the civic centre, Accra: offices of the Accra Town Council (left) and the Bank of Ghana (right) (see p. 152).

PLATE 19*b*. The fishing village of Anomabu. Note the ovens for smoking fish (see pp. 82 and 156).

PLATE 20*a*. Onion farming in the Keta-Anloga area. The crops are watered regularly from wells located on the farms (see p. 160).

PLATE 20*b*. The Volta dam at Akosombo in the Ajena gorge (see p. 104). Below the dam on the far side can be seen the penstocks and the power-house, while at the nearer end are the slipways where the overflow from the lake will pass. The dam began to fill on 8 February 1965 and the generation of electricity started on 22 January 1966 (see pp. 104, 161).

PLATE 21*a*. The Ayimensa–Aburi road in the Akwapim-Togo ranges (see p. 168).

PLATE 21*b*. Kumasi, the 'Garden City of West Africa' (see p. 176).

PLATE 22*a*. Transport on the Keta Lagoon. Many more boats and people can be seen on market days (see p. 160).

PLATE 22*b*. A view of Biakpa and the Amedzofe Pass (see p. 168).

PLATE 23*a*. A village scene in the Bawku area, Northern Region. Note tobacco plants in the foreground and the typical parkland savanna vegetation of these parts in the background (see pp. 51 and 199).

PLATE 23*b*. Making yam mounds in the Tamale area. In the background is a typical view of the savanna vegetation, which is here dominated by trees and truly deserves the description 'orchard bush' (see pp. 51 and 196).

PLATE 24. Penned cattle in a Navrongo compound, Northern Region (see p. 199).

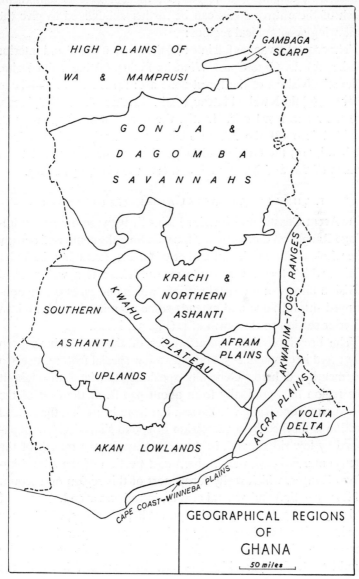

HIGH PLAINS OF WA & MAMPRUSI

GAMBAGA SCARP

GONJA & DAGOMBA SAVANNAHS

KWAHU PLATEAU

KRACHI & NORTHERN ASHANTI

AKWAPIM-TOGO RANGES

SOUTHERN ASHANTI UPLANDS

AFRAM PLAINS

ACCRA PLAINS

VOLTA DELTA

AKAN LOWLANDS

CAPE COAST-WINNEBA PLAINS

GEOGRAPHICAL REGIONS OF GHANA

50 miles

Fig. 31

landforms, climate and vegetation, to economic development, each of these three zones can be further subdivided to give the following geographical regions:

The coastal savannas fall into: (1) the Accra Coastal and Interior Plains, (2) the Cape Coast–Winneba Plains, (3) the Volta Delta. The subdivisions of the forest zone are: (4) the Akwapim-Togo Ranges, (5) the Kwahu Plateau, (6) the Southern Ashanti Uplands, (7) the Akan Lowlands. Lastly, the northern savannas may be divided into (8) the Afram Plains, (9) Krachi and Northern Ashanti, (10) the Gonja and Dagomba Savannas, (11) the High Plains of Wa and Mamprusi, and (12) the Gambaga Scarp.

I. THE ACCRA COASTAL AND INTERIOR PLAINS

The Accra Coastal and Interior Plains lie between the Akwapim-Togo Ranges on the north and the sea along the south and occupy the whole of the south-east corner of Ghana, excluding the Volta Delta, which forms a separate region. There is a well-marked division into two: a coastal section, which embraces the lagoon-fringed littoral zone and extends some 10 miles inland, and an interior section to the north of it (Fig. 32, inset).

The broad physical characteristics of the region have been discussed in chapters 2–5, and only a few special features need to be mentioned here. Generally speaking, the land throughout the region falls gradually from about 500 ft. at the foot of the Akwapim-Togo Ranges to the sea. Far from being flat, the coastal section is marked by a succession of spoon-shaped valleys separated by low ridges, and, in the area between the mouth of the Densu and Pokoasi, the southernmost portion of the Akwapim-Togo Ranges, which really forms part of this region on account of its vegetation and general aridity, introduces even bolder relief (Figs. 32 and 33). Many of the spoon-shaped valleys, which carry the intermittent drainage of the plains, are swampy during the wet season and their mouths are frequently blocked along the sea by sand-bars to form brackish lagoons. In areas of fairly resistant rocks, e.g. east of Accra harbour, the shore is rocky and cliffed, but elsewhere there is a fairly gradual sandy slope to the sea.

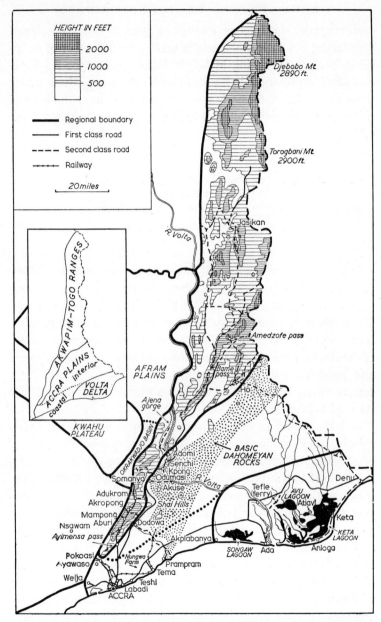

Fig. 32. The Accra Plains, the Volta Delta and the Akwapim-Togo Ranges.

In contrast, the Interior Plains are generally flat and almost featureless; but their monotony is broken by a number of steep-sided inselbergs, ranging in height from 900 to 1500 ft. Especially striking are those in the Shai and Krobo areas, whose strong defensive positions formerly made them notorious as the seats of raiding communities much dreaded by people travelling across the plains.

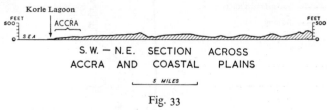

S. W. — N. E. SECTION ACROSS
ACCRA AND COASTAL PLAINS

Fig. 33

One striking characteristic of this region is the anomalously low rainfall. In the interior section the annual amount varies between 35 and 45 in., but in the Coastal Plains it rarely exceeds 35 in. The result is that the Interior Plains have a thicker cover of bush, fewer ant-hills and richer soils than the more open grassy scrub of the coastal section. Also, such trees as mangoes, coconut palms and baobabs, which are common in the coastal section, are comparatively rare in the wetter, northern section near the Akwapim-Togo Ranges.

Outside the urban centres the main human activities are agriculture, stock raising and fishing. Agriculture is almost exclusively of the shifting type, though near Accra a type of fixed farming employing farmyard droppings is practised on a very limited scale. The usual crops are cassava (the most widespread), maize, peppers, tomatoes, okros and garden eggs (Plate 18 a). These crops are grown primarily for local consumption and for sale in the larger and coastal settlements. The farms are usually not larger than one or two acres and are grouped round small villages dotting the plains or strung along motor roads for ease of communication with buying centres within the locality. Firing of the grass usually precedes farming operations and the trees killed by the fires provide a valuable source of firewood.

These plains, especially the drier coastal section, have the advantage of being fairly free from tsetse and are therefore suitable for livestock breeding. The best pastures, consisting of short Guinea grass, are in the eastern section, between Teshie and Ada, but the general shortage of water here, as in other parts of the Coastal Plains, is a serious drawback. Nevertheless, the industry continues to make great strides. A government veterinary station at Nungwa provides valuable technical assistance for the breeders of livestock, and since 1934 rinderpest, a dangerous cattle disease, has been virtually wiped out from the region.[1] Other animals, such as poultry, goats, pigs and some sheep, are reared, but on a much smaller scale.

Even more important than agriculture and livestock breeding is fishing, which takes place along the whole stretch of coast as well as in the coastal lagoons and along the lower Volta within the Interior Plains. Even Accra, which is primarily a commercial and administrative town, has a fishing population of over 2000. Other prominent centres of the industry are Labadi, Teshie, Tema and Prampram.

Another industry, which has been given a new impetus recently by the extensive building and road-making within the region, is quarrying. Of particular importance for road-making are the ironstone concretions found in the widespread lateritic rocks. Building stone is derived chiefly from the hard quartzites of the Togo series of rocks and the gneisses of the Dahomeyan series (see chapter 2). These gneisses have recently been intensively exploited in the Shai inselbergs for the construction of the new harbour at Tema.

In no other region is urban life felt as much as it is here. In the eastern section of the Plains beyond the Volta the centre to which people are naturally attracted is Keta, but west of the Volta the Plains are completely dominated by the town of Accra, which is at once the capital of Ghana, the largest commercial centre, a focus for international air lines, and the former leading roadstead

[1] See *Report on the Livestock Industry of the Eastern Province*, by A. Fulton (Gold Coast, 1935).

port, handling a volume of trade surpassed only by Takoradi. Most of the agricultural produce of the Plains and a large area far beyond pours daily into Accra by road and rail to feed its population of over 337,000. In addition to its other functions, Accra has a large variety of small industries, notably furniture making, brick and tile making, the manufacture of nails from imported wire, salt making, fruit and fish canning, and brewing.

Considering its modest beginnings only a few centuries ago and its location in an earthquake zone, the growth of Accra to its present position and size is quite remarkable. About the end of the sixteenth century, when a section of the Ga people, whose main seat was at Ayawaso 10 miles further inland, came to live at Accra, it formed only a small village on the eastern shore of the Korle lagoon. Gradually, Accra's advantageous position for trade with the nearby European forts and its comparative security from attack by the Akwamus, who were a menace at Ayawaso, attracted more people, until eventually most of the Gas came to live there. The inhabitants engaged in trade, farming and lagoon fishing. It was not until the middle of the eighteenth century, when the Fantis introduced them to the art, that they took up sea fishing.

As a trading centre, Accra was at first overshadowed by the ports of Ada and Prampram and by such inland centres as Dodowa and Akuse further east, although its forts gave it special prominence in the slave trade. After the abolition of slavery in 1807 it lost this advantage, but gained a new importance when it was chosen in 1876 to supersede Cape Coast as the administrative capital of the British government. One reason for the choice was the drier climate and the comparative absence of tsetse fly, which made the use of animal transport possible at Accra. By the end of the nineteenth century the town had practically filled the angle of land between the Korle lagoon and the sea, and a suburb for European officials and government offices had come into being at Victoriaborg, between Accra proper and Christiansborg castle.

The construction of the Accra–Kumasi railway between 1905 and 1923 and the general economic prosperity brought about by the cocoa industry, which had by this time overshadowed the earlier palm-oil industry, turned attention away from Ada, Prampram, Dodowa and Akuse and focused it on Accra. The old town expanded northwards and fresh suburbs developed at Adabraka and across the lagoon at Korle Gonno, where a modern hospital had been built. Also, a new residential suburb—the Ridge—was built north of Victoriaborg to house the ever-growing number of European officials.

Alongside the physical expansion of Accra, several improvements took place in its internal layout or 'morphology' and in its sanitation. In the newer parts streets and drains were properly planned from the very outset, but even in the older parts, where houses were of poor construction and ill arranged, attempts were made to widen and straighten the main streets, which had been quite adequate for the era of horses and mule-drawn carts but were unsuitable for motor traffic. Of special importance for the health of the population was the introduction in 1915 of a piped water supply from the Weija Waterworks on the Densu. Before then the only source of water had been wells and periodical rain-water.

Expansion since has been quite considerable. The town today (Fig. 34) extends for a distance of six miles or more from the original nucleus in the vicinity of James Fort and Ussher Fort and includes many settlements like Christiansborg and Labadi that were formerly separate entities. Equally striking has been the growth of the population: 16,267 in 1891, 26,622 in 1901, 29,602 in 1911, 42,803 in 1921, 60,726 in 1931 and 135,926 in 1948. This growth continues, and since the Second World War over-population and traffic congestion have become serious problems within the municipality. In 1960 the population had reached 337,828.

However, vigorous efforts are being made to tackle these problems and to reshape Accra for its new role as capital of an independent country. Several housing estates have been built on the fringes of the city and some of the essential services now concentrated in the old, overcrowded centre are being scattered among the suburbs. There are also significant changes in architecture, and many of the recently erected civic and commercial buildings run into several storeys and stand well above the single and two-storey buildings that were formerly the rule. These developments are best illustrated in the region of Kwame Nkrumah

Fig. 34

Avenue and in the civic centre, between the Post Office and Parliament Buildings (Plates 18*b*, 19*a*).

Another notable change which has taken place recently in the morphology of Accra has been the emergence of an industrial zone along the Ring Road between Kaneshie and Accra New Town. This area lies close to the Korle lagoon and its affluent, the Odaw river, and its development has been hampered in the past by flooding during the heavy rains. However, measures are now being taken to control this problem and render the lagoon a more effective outlet into the sea.

The other large settlements in the region are found either along the sea or along the Accra–Dodowa–Senchi road. The famous educational centre of Achimota and the new University of Ghana site at Legon, eight miles north of Accra, are now regarded as part of the Accra municipality. Seventeen miles east of Accra is the new port of Tema, which is fast developing into a major industrial centre (see chapter 10). Its population in 1960 was 22,823.

Among the places along the Accra–Dodowa–Senchi road may be mentioned Dodowa, which for many years was the seat of the Joint Provincial Council of Chiefs, and before then was a leading commercial centre serving the port of Prampram. A few miles east of Dodowa is the Krobo town of Somanya, followed by a number of smaller but busy commercial and market centres. Odumasi, which is one of the Krobo capitals, is noted for its many schools and colleges. On the Volta are Akuse, still an important commercial centre, though not quite as busy as it was fifty years ago when the Volta was a busy trade artery, Senchi and Kpong. Senchi is only a small settlement, which owes its existence entirely to the ferry, which, until the opening in 1957 of the Volta bridge at Adomi, a few miles to the north, provided the only direct link in the region for communications between Accra and the Volta Region. Kpong, formerly an important commercial town, has greatly declined and now serves as a veterinary centre.

Apart from the larger settlements, the Accra Coastal and Interior Plains contain several smaller ones. Their positions are determined mainly by the availability of water, communications and other special economic advantages, such as situation along the sea. Consequently, the number of settlements is comparatively large in the 'spring zone' at the foot of the Akwapim-Togo Ranges, along the main roads and along the sea. Elsewhere, settlements usually occur only near wells or water-holes scattered over the Plains or along pipelines like that between Accra and Achimota, where regular water supply is assured.

This region has recently attracted a great deal of attention because of the Volta Aluminium Project, which will operate largely within its boundaries (see chapter 8). In addition to the smelter at Tema, it is proposed to intensify agriculture in certain parts of the Plains by means of irrigation, and experiments are already in progress at the University of Ghana's agricultural stations at Kpong and Nungwa to determine how best the land can be used. In particular, the heavy black clays or Akuse soils, as they are called, which develop over the basic gneisses of the Dahomeyan series in the central part of the region, are being studied to assess their full potentialities. They are considered to be among the most fertile soils in the country, but so far their stiffness and tendency to dry out rapidly and crack during the dry season have prevented them from being effectively used for agriculture.

2. THE CAPE COAST–WINNEBA PLAINS

The Cape Coast–Winneba Plains form a narrow zone of about 5–10 miles in width extending along the coast between Weija and Sekondi (Fig. 35). They are thus really a westward extension of the Accra Plains, which they closely resemble in climate and vegetation. The section east of Saltpond is more like the Accra Coastal Plains, while the wetter section to the west is more comparable with the Interior Plains. Its vegetation consists predominantly of bush, and grass is conspicuous only around the larger settlements, where prolonged farming and burning have destroyed the bush. On the whole the relief is more undulating than in the Accra Plains and the granite, which underlies most of the region, gives rise to typical rounded hills separated by wide valleys.

The region is tsetse-infested and cattle breeding is therefore unimportant. The main occupations are farming and fishing. The area west of Saltpond is, generally speaking, much more developed agriculturally than the drier eastern section, which until the construction of the Accra–Winneba road a few years ago was further handicapped by poor accessibility and lack of good internal communications. The farm products found in the Accra Plains are grown throughout this region, but in the western half such forest crops as plantains and cocoyams are also found.

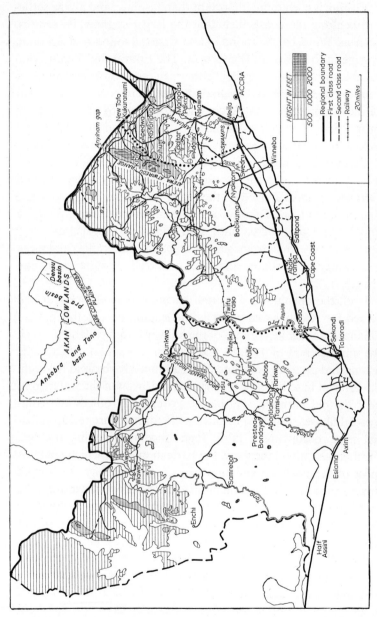

Fig. 35. The Cape Coast–Winneba Plains and the Akan Lowlands.

Fishing is even more important than farming, and all the settlements along the coast, including the larger commercial centres, such as Winneba, Saltpond, Cape Coast, Elmina and Sekondi, engage in the industry (Plate 19b). The Effutus and Fantis, who inhabit the area, are excellent fishermen, and whole communities can frequently be found even along the Accra coast at the height of the fishing season. At Accra itself they used to provide a large proportion of the crews of surf boats employed in loading and unloading ocean-going vessels in the now defunct roadstead port.

Commerce is highly developed in this part of Ghana and has a long history going back to the fifteenth century, when the first European traders arrived on the coast. Winneba, Saltpond, Cape Coast, Sekondi and Takoradi are all commercial centres. Winneba and Cape Coast were, until 1961, open surf ports, handling comparatively small tonnages of cargo, but Takoradi is a modern well-equipped harbour and the country's leading port (see chapter 10).

Until the opening of Takoradi harbour in 1928, Sekondi had served for twenty-seven years as the leading port in this part of Ghana and the sole terminus of the railway leading inland through the mining areas of Tarkwa and Obuasi to Kumasi. Today only fishing and pleasure boats use the abandoned harbour at Sekondi, but a naval base is being constructed nearby. On the waterfront, near the old harbour, are the old government offices and commercial houses, followed inland by the former European residential area, occupying a fairly high ridge overlooking the sea. Further west along the sea is the African quarter, which contains most of the town's population of 34,513. Buildings reach right down to the sea, and although this has the effect of exposing the corrugated iron roofs of most of the older houses to rapid decay due to the salt-charged sea breeze, it gives Sekondi a sea-front that is potentially one of the most attractive in Ghana.

Six miles west of Sekondi is Takoradi. Originally, the two places were quite separate physically, but there are now so many buildings in the intervening area that they are regarded as a single municipality and often described as Sekondi-Takoradi. Takoradi

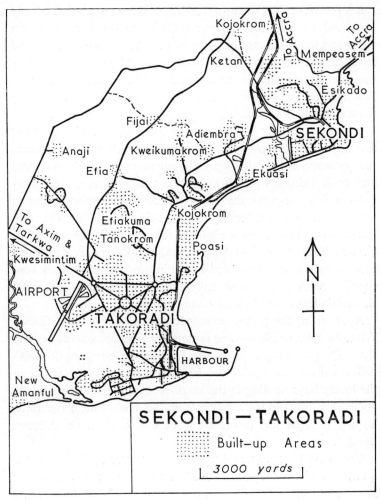

Fig. 36

is solely the creation of the harbour, and there is an obvious newness about the town, whose cosmopolitan population of 40,937 displays all the characteristics of an unsettled community. It has grown rapidly since 1931, when it had a population of only 5478, and still continues to expand. Owing to its very recent origin it has had the advantage of a proper plan to shape its growth and has therefore few of the problems of uncontrolled growth faced by the other large centres in the region (Fig. 36). Besides the harbour Takoradi has an airport, which played a prominent role during the war but is now used solely by the internal air services.

Industrial activity is growing within the region. The assembly and repair of locomotives and railway coaches takes place at the government Location works barely two miles from Takoradi, and both Takoradi and Sekondi have a number of large saw-mills, which are particularly well placed as all exports of sawn timber and logs pass through Takoradi. In addition, Takoradi has a paper factory and a cigarette factory, while Sekondi has a boat-building factory. At Abakrampa, near Cape Coast, a British firm owns a small lime-juice extraction industry, which is kept supplied with fruit grown largely by local farmers (Fig. 21); Komenda has a sugar factory and Elmina has salt works.

Apart from the purely economic activities, the Cape Coast–Winneba Plains have become famous for their coastal resorts and their old, picturesque fort towns. Increasing numbers of week-end visitors make use of the bathing facilities to be found in the lovely bays nestling in the lee of rocky headlands, frequently commanded by old forts dating from the days of the slave trade. Typical of these fort towns are Cape Coast, Elmina and Senya Beraku.

Cape Coast (pop. 41,230) was for many years the British head-quarters and capital of the country, until it was superseded by Accra in 1876. It has played a prominent role in the history and political life of Ghana, and is today the administrative capital of the Central Region as well as a centre of education, with several well-known schools and a University College. The historic Cape Coast Castle almost dominates the town by its massiveness,but its main function today is to provide offices for various government departments. In the lee of the castle lies the landing beach formerly used by surf boats serving the roadstead port.

Another defunct roadstead port in the region is Winneba (pop. 25,376). As a port Winneba served as outlet and inlet for a rich hinterland embracing the area around Swedru, but the commercial activity which once made it such a busy centre has continued to decline. It was expected that the new road which links the town direct with Accra would bring about a revival, but this has not occurred.

North of the coastal towns and fishing villages, the Cape Coast–Winneba Plains contain numerous small agricultural settlements. As there is no pronounced scarcity of water, except perhaps in the section east of Saltpond, most of these settlements are located where communications are favourable.

3. THE VOLTA DELTA

Over the centuries the Volta has built a huge delta at its mouth, between Akplabanya in the west and Denu in the east. Sandbars have blocked the mouth of the river, splitting it into numerous channels. Similarly, the mouths of a number of smaller streams entering the sea here have been blocked to produce a maze of lagoons of varying sizes, of which the largest are the Songaw and Keta lagoons near the sea and the Avu lagoon further inland.

The land is quite flat. The rainfall is only slightly higher than that of the Accra Coastal Plains, and the vegetation is predominantly grass, dotted with fan palms. Along the coast are dense groves of coconut palms, which form the basis of a prosperous copra industry. Around Dzodze, further inland, is an important oil-palm industry.

As is to be expected, the soils consist of sands and clays of recent age, which have been deposited by the rivers. Although they are somewhat dry away from the water-courses and lagoons, they produce fairly useful and easily worked soils for agriculture. Cassava is widely grown and so are maize, the other local staple, and beans, peppers, garden eggs and okros. Between Keta and

Anloga occurs a type of irrigated farming which is really gardening of a very special kind. The droppings of bats from old ruins and fish waste are carefully worked into the soil for the cultivation of a type of small onion, known as shallots (Plate 20a). These are produced in large quantities and find a ready sale all over Ghana.

The chief occupation of the people, however, is fishing, both in the sea and in the lagoons. Dried, salted fish is one of the region's main exports to other parts of Ghana. Another export is salt, which is obtained from the lagoons during the dry season.

The abundance of water, swamps and lagoons makes road communications difficult in this region (Plate 22a). The road from Accra to Keta, for example, makes a huge detour inland just before reaching Ada and eventually approaches Keta from the east along the narrow spit on which the town stands (Fig. 32). The ferry at Tefle, which takes traffic across the Volta, is thus of critical importance in the local system of communications, the more so as the same route provides the most direct road link between Ghana and Western Nigeria, through Lome in Togoland. Formerly, the now defunct ferry at Ada provided a more direct, but less reliable, route between Accra and Keta.

Almost all the settlements in the delta region are found either in the north, along the main road, or in the south, along the narrow spit between the sea and Keta lagoon. The settlements in the south thus have a double water frontage. Although this is an asset for the fishing industry, the spit is much too narrow to provide a satisfactory site for settlements that are in process of expansion. It has proved particularly unsatisfactory for Keta, which is continually threatened with extinction by inroads from the sea, but is yet prevented by the lagoon on the other side of the spit from retreating further inland.

Keta is the administrative and commercial centre of this region and formerly a minor roadstead port (see chapter 10). In 1960 its population was 16,719, the largest of any settlement within the region. Other fairly large settlements are Anloga (pop. 11,038), which contains a considerable farming population despite its situation along the sea, and Atiavi (pop. 2811) on the northern shore of the Keta lagoon. Ada, once an important port at the mouth of the Volta, is today quite an insignificant place, containing a population of only 3332.

4. THE AKWAPIM-TOGO RANGES

Physically, the Akwapim-Togo Ranges form one of the most striking regions of Ghana. Seen from the Accra Plains the ranges stand out clearly against the sky (Plate 3a). The region comprises the whole of the highland area extending roughly in a north-easterly direction from Pokoasi, a few miles north of Accra, to the Togoland boundary in the region of Dutukpene and Kadjebi in the Krachi district (Fig. 32). Beyond this point it continues through Togo and Dahomey to the Niger river. French geographers usually refer to the whole of these ranges, including the southernmost portion between Pokoasi and the sea, as the 'Togo-Atakora Mountains', but the term 'Akwapim-Togo Ranges' is a convenient name for the portion lying within Ghana.

These ranges do not form a simple feature, but are composed of a complex of folds which change their character from south to north. In Akwapim, particularly, the folding is very confused, and the complex way in which the different beds of rock lie on top of one another can be seen quite clearly in the roadside cutting between Ayimensa and Aburi.

The section between the sea and Kpandu has a south-west to north-east trend and consists mostly of rocks of the Togo series, but north of Kpandu the trend is more nearly from south to north and the rocks belong to the Buem series. Also, many of the prominent heights contain volcanic rocks, mostly basalt. The descent from the Ranges to the Accra Interior Plains in the south and to the Afram Plains in the north is sometimes steep, and cliffs suggesting extensive fracturing of the rocks or even local faulting occur in a number of places.

The Volta cuts across the ranges in a deep, narrow gorge at Ajena (Fig. 37 and Plate 20b). The section west of the gorge forms the Akwapim section, while that to the east forms the Togo section. In the Akwapim section, which has an average height of 1500 ft., the ranges are generally higher and the valleys deeper and narrower than in the section between the Volta and Kpandu. Here, the ridges are quite low and are separated by broad valleys. Between Kpandu and Dutukpene, however, the folds become more complex and the ranges are much higher, some attaining almost 3000 ft. in places. Two particularly prominent peaks here are Torogbani (2900 ft.), near Mpeyo, and Djebobo (2890 ft.), a few miles east of Kadjebi.

Throughout the region farming is the leading occupation. The usual forest crops, such as plantains, cocoyams, yams, and others of wider distribution like cassava, maize, peppers, garden eggs, okros and beans of various kinds are found, but in the Krachi section, in the extreme north, these give way to yams, rice and other crops more suited to the drier conditions of the area. The Akwapim and Togo areas, south of Krachi, also contain large number of palm trees, which provide palm oil and palm wine. In the late nineteenth century and during the early years of the present century, when palm oil was the leading export of Ghana, this region formed an important producer, and palm oil still features prominently as a local item of diet.

Following the decline of the palm-oil industry, Akwapim became the leading cocoa-producing area in Ghana and was in fact the place where the crop was first cultivated commercially. Today, soil impoverishment and disease have virtually wiped out the industry and led to a large-scale movement of Akwapim farmers westward into the rich forest lands of Akim and Ashanti, now the chief cocoa-producing areas in the country. In contrast, the Volta Region (formerly Togoland)—especially around Ho and also between Kpandu and Jasikan—is still an important producer of cocoa. Coffee growing, which the Germans established before they lost the territory to Britain in 1918, is also quite significant, although other parts of Ghana such as Brong-Ahafo are now important producers.

With the exception of the Krachi area, which exports large quantities of yams to other parts of the country, cocoa and coffee from the Volta Region represent the only major cash crops from the

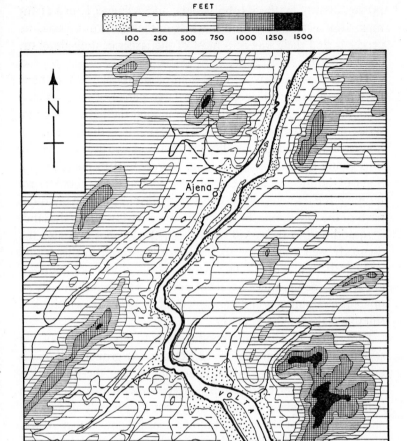

FEET

100 250 500 750 1000 1250 1500

VOLTA GORGE AT AJENA

2 MILES

Fig. 37

entire region. Indeed, some places in Akwapim now obtain a
considerable proportion of their foodstuffs from the basin of the
Pawmpawm, a tributary of the Afram, between Okrakwadjo
and Asesewa. This area, which lies between the Akwapim-Togo
Ranges and the eastern end of the Kwahu Plateau, is occupied

predominantly by the Krobo people, and Asesewa is one of the most famous and busy food markets in the whole of Ghana. Its products find their way into most of the larger centres along the coast and in the forest zone.

The Krobos have evolved a system of farming known as 'huza farming'. A group of people buy a large parcel of land, usually adjoining a stream, and divide it up among the individuals in a series of narrow strips, each with a frontage along the stream. The houses of the individual families are usually placed near the stream, thus giving rise to a series of long, narrow settlements (Fig. 26). Some of the 'huza' villages extend for as long as three miles.[1] 'Huza farming' is based on shifting cultivation, just like farming in other parts of the forest zone, but more intensive use is made of the land.

In addition to their skill as farmers, the Krobos and also the Shais are well known for their pottery, and both in this region and in other parts of Ghana where Krobo and Shai communities are settled they produce excellent pottery. This is particularly so in areas containing granite and such rocks as gneiss, which yield suitable clays for the industry.

Differences in economic conditions between one part of the region and another are closely reflected in the growth and distribution of population. In the Akwapim section the population density is in the region of 200 persons per square mile. This figure is one of the highest in the country, but it is mainly due to the past prosperity of the area. The 1960 census showed that Akwapim's population is increasing so slowly now as to indicate a decline in the total population in the near future. The decline in agriculture and the almost complete lack of commercial opportunities have caused a drifting away of young people into other parts of the country, and in most of the settlements there is an unusually large proportion of children and old people.

Between Akwapim and Ho the population density is not so great, but the same signs of decline are present. North of Ho, as far as Jasikan, however, where cocoa is important, the population

[1] See 'The Agricultural System of the Manya Krobo of the Gold Coast', by M. J. Field, *Africa*, vol. xiv (1943).

is growing rapidly, although the density is as yet much smaller than in the south. But there is a sharp drop in the Krachi area, which is among the least densely populated parts of Ghana (see chapter 9 and also Fig. 25*a* and *b*).

A striking feature about the distribution of settlements in the region is that in Akwapim the larger settlements lie mostly on the

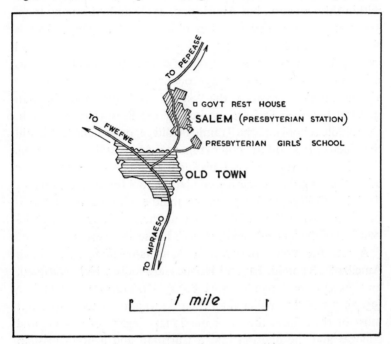

Fig. 38. Abetifi (showing 'twin' development).

narrow mountain ridge, while in the Togo section they are more usually in the valleys. One explanation may be that the narrower valleys in Akwapim are so damp and misty that they have been deliberately avoided,[1] but there is no doubt that the stronger defensive positions of the mountain sites were deliberately sought by the Akwapims in the early days of inter-tribal warfare.

Missionary activity, dating back in some places well over a

[1] See *Our Homeland, Book I: South-East Gold Coast*, by D. A. Chapman (Achimota, 1943).

hundred years, has been a strong factor in the social life of both Akwapim and Togoland, although most of the settlements were in existence long before the arrival of the missionaries. Churches and schools, often situated in a special 'mission quarter', known as 'Salem', are familiar features in all the larger settlements (Fig. 38). Practically all the 'ridge towns' in Akwapim come within this category, but Aburi (pop. 4715) and Akropong (pop. 5606) may be regarded as typical examples. Akropong, which is the seat of the Paramount Chief and, therefore, the divisional capital, has a large Training College dating from 1828 as well as a famous middle school and a secondary school. There is now no visible division between the 'Salem' and the non-Christian quarter, but their foci are marked by the Presbyterian Church, the middle school and the Training College, on the one hand, and the chief's house on the other (Fig. 39). Aburi still maintains the tradition begun by the Basel missionaries of being a centre for the education of girls and has a secondary school for girls, a women's Training College, and two famous middle schools. As at Akropong, the two sections of the 'town' are now visually one, but the two foci of the 'Salem' and the chief's house are present.

Across the Volta, the chief settlements—Anum, Boso, Peki, Amedzofe, Kpandu, Ho and Hohoe—are more widely scattered, and, except for Kpandu (pop. 8070), Ho (14,519) and Hohoe (9502), generally smaller than their Akwapim counterparts. But most of them have the same missionary legacy of schools and colleges and the division into a Christian and a non-Christian quarter.

On account of their pleasant climate and attractive scenery, many of the mountain 'towns' in the region, in particular Aburi, Anum and Amedzofe, have developed into popular 'hill stations', much frequented by tourists. Mampong (4449) in Akwapim deserves special mention as the home of Tetteh Quashie and the place where he planted his first cocoa seedlings. It is commercially the most important of the Akwapim 'ridge towns' or 'home towns', as they are more popularly known locally, but its present activity is greatly reduced and it lives mainly on its past reputation and

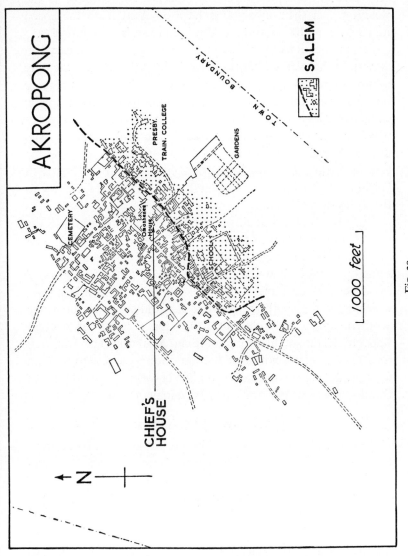

AKROPONG

SALEM

TOWN BOUNDARY

PRESBY.
TRAIN. COLLEGE

GARDENS

CEMETERY

Omanhene's
HOUSE

SCHOOL

1000 feet

Fig. 39

CHIEF'S
HOUSE

N

prosperity. The large, impressive buildings to be found there and elsewhere in Akwapim, especially Aburi, are a reflection of the wealth which their inhabitants have amassed from the cocoa industry. Another important Akwapim town is Larteh (6381). Communications in this mountainous region are not easy. In Akwapim the Accra–Koforidua road along the ridge is the only important routeway, but across the Volta the roads are more numerous and follow the valleys. A few transverse roads follow suitable passes or routes in the mountains, the most important of which are the Ayimensa–Aburi road (Plate 21 a), the Bame pass and the Amedzofe pass (Plate 22 b). No important road serves the Krachi section of the region, although a road to the Northern Region formerly passed through Kete-Krachi not far away to the west on the Volta.

These roads play a vital role in connecting the region with the larger commercial centres nearby. The Volta Region is fortunate in having the commercial centres of Ho, Kpandu and Hohoe actually within its boundaries, but in Akwapim the 'ridge towns' are dependent on centres outside, such as Accra and Nsawam, which serve the southern part, and Koforidua, which serves the northern areas. The roads to Koforidua descend the western slopes of the ranges through Mamfe and Adukrom. The Adukrom road is of special significance because it offers access to the rich food-producing Okrakwadjo basin, between the villages of Okrakwadjo and Asesewa in the Pawmpawm valley.

5. THE KWAHU PLATEAU

The Kwahu Plateau, which stretches for some 120 miles between Koforidua in the east and Wenchi in north-western Ashanti, corresponds to the southern, elevated edge of the Voltaian basin (see chapter 2). The region is so named because, although large parts in the east and west lie in Akim Abuakwa and in Ashanti, the central and best-known section falls within Kwahu. The eastern end of the Plateau is separated from the Akwapim-Togo Ranges by the fertile Okrakwadjo basin (see above and Fig. 40).

The Plateau is composed largely of horizontal or only slightly

168

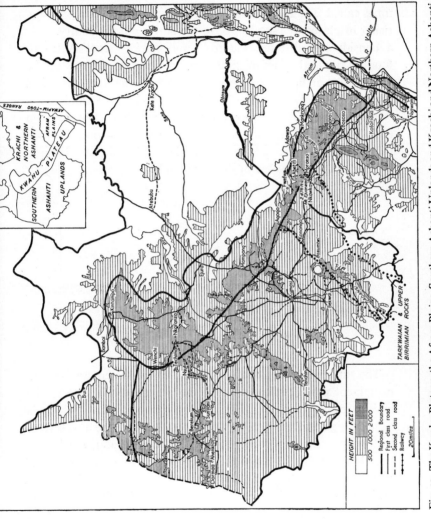

Fig. 40. The Kwahu Plateau, the Afram Plains, Southern Ashanti Uplands and Krachi and Northern Ashanti.

folded Upper Voltaian sandstones. Its average elevation is about 1500 ft., and both its northern and southern boundaries are marked by erosional scarps (Fig. 41). The southern scarp, some-times called 'The Koforidua-Wenchi Scarp', is especially striking, rising in places to 1500 ft. above the surrounding country. For a considerable distance the road and railway from Accra to Kumasi run at the foot of this scarp, and impressive views can be gained of it at Bososo and Nkawkaw, where the scarp face rises almost sheer, revealing the horizontal strata of the sandstones. Around Wenchi the scarp is much less prominent. The scarp on the northern or inner side of the Plateau is not as prominent as that on the southern side, but near Ejura it is quite striking and affords an excellent view of the Voltaian basin beyond.

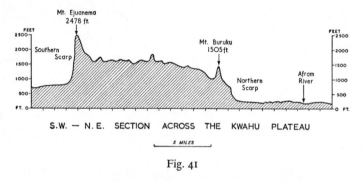

S.W. — N. E. SECTION ACROSS THE KWAHU PLATEAU

Fig. 41

The surface of the plateau itself is highly dissected, and several prominent peaks stick out above the general level. One of the highest peaks is Mount Ejuanema, near Nkawkaw, which is 2478 ft. high and has rich bauxite deposits. There are also several picturesque masses of rock, such as Buruku in Kwahu, which have been left standing here and there above the surface as a result of erosion aided by the joints in the sandstones. Practically all the drainage is into the Afram and ultimately into the Volta.

Physically, the Kwahu Plateau is one of the most important dividing features in Ghana. It forms the principal watershed of the country, dividing the Birim, Pra, Ofin, Tano and other rivers which flow south into the sea from the Afram, Pru and other rivers flowing into the Volta. It also forms the northern rampart of the forest country lying south of it. The whole plateau is covered with a deciduous type of forest similar to that found in the Akwapim-Togo Ranges. Although large areas of this forest have been destroyed as a result of farming and burning, there are many forest reserves on the plateau, which protect the headwaters of the rivers flowing from it and help to shield the whole of the forest country to the south against the dry Harmattan winds from the north-east.

Everywhere the chief human occupation is farming of the forest type found in the Akwapim-Togo Ranges. In the Kwahu and Akim sections cocoa is not now as important as food growing, although recently Kwahu farmers have begun to develop the northern slopes between Adawso and Mankrong. This area has considerable possibilities, but is still seriously handicapped by the lack of good communications. In the lowland bay around the village of Fwefwe in Kwahu, where the forest begins to give way to the savanna of the Afram Plains, large quantities of onions and tiger nuts are cultivated. West of Kwahu lies the Ashanti section of the plateau. Here, in addition to food farming, cocoa is important, especially between Mampong and Wenchi.

On the whole, the Kwahu Plateau is poorly served with roads, which are not easy to construct owing to the steepness of the scarps. Only in the region of Mpraeso in Kwahu and Mampong in Ashanti are the really difficult parts penetrated by important roads. The two famous missionary centres of Bogoro and Agogo, respectively in Akim Abuakwa and Ashanti, are reached by roads which ascend the scarp but do not continue across the whole width of the plateau. The Mpraeso road continues to the Afram valley, while the Mampong road continues through Ejura as the Great North Road. A number of other roads radiating northwards from Kumasi across the lower, western end of the plateau serve the cocoa lands of this area. The most notable of these is the Kumasi–Wenchi road, which provides another, though less important, route to the north. The Mampong and Wenchi roads are linked together by shorter roads through Nkoranza, Kintampo and Techiman.

The uneven character of economic development in the region is reflected in the population density, which is generally low. Between Koforidua and Agogo it averages from 100 to 200 persons per square mile, although few places in fact approach the higher figure. North of Agogo the density falls from 100 to 50 persons per square miles. However, the western section is undergoing vigorous economic development, and there are now about five settlements there with over 3000 inhabitants in contrast with the position in 1948 when only two settlements there were in this category as compared with five settlements in the eastern section (Table 12).

Eastern section		Western section	
Town	*Population*	*Town*	*Population*
Mpraeso	3346	Wenchi	3812
Abetifi	4030	Mampong	3948
Nkwatia	3547		
Begoro	5061		
Agogo	4744		

Table 12. *Distribution of settlements with over 3000 inhabitants in 1948*

Most of the larger centres in the eastern section are concentrated within a comparatively small area in Kwahu (Fig. 25). This brings out an interesting feature of the geography of Kwahu, which extends northward to include practically the whole of the Afram Plains, but yet has most of its population concentrated on the plateau on account of the better prospects it offers at present for agriculture. Mpraeso (pop. 5193) is the chief commercial and route centre in Kwahu after Nkawkaw (pop. 15,627), which lies at the foot of the plateau, but may for all practical purposes be included with it, since they are closely linked together commercially, and many of the farming community at Nkawkaw have their lands within the plateau region. Nkawkaw lies on the road and railway between Accra and Kumasi, and may be regarded as the southern gateway of Kwahu.

Despite their structural differences, the Kwahu Plateau contains many features which resemble those of the Akwapim-Togo

Ranges. In particular, the comparatively cool climate due to the high altitude attracted missionary enterprise in much the same way as in Akwapim and the Volta Region. Begoro, Abetifi, Agogo and Mampong are all old and active centres of religious education and contain well-known schools and colleges. In all of them the dual development of Christian and non-Christian sections within the same settlement is clearly exemplified (Fig. 38), and their attractive scenery and cool climate have made them popular with tourists, especially Europeans.

6. THE SOUTHERN ASHANTI UPLANDS

The Southern Ashanti Uplands form, economically, perhaps the most important region in Ghana, combining both mineral and agricultural wealth as well as considerable urban and commercial development. The region, which coincides with the upper or northern, higher section of the structural unit described in chapter 2 as 'The Akan Dissected Peneplain', lies wholly within Ashanti and extends from the foot of the Kwahu Plateau in the north to the northern boundary of the Western and Eastern Regions of Ghana. Its natural focus is Kumasi, on which all the main roads and the railways converge.

The land slopes gently from about 1000 ft. in the north to 500 ft. in the south but, true to its character as a dissected peneplain, it contains several hills and ranges standing above the general level and rising in some places to between 1500 and 2500 ft. above sea level. Two of the most prominent of these ranges are the Adansi Mountains, extending south-westwards from Lake Bosumtwi, and the range between Nsuta and Bibiani, 30 miles west of Kumasi. This north-east to south-west trend, which is repeated by almost all the other ranges in the region (Fig. 40), appears to correspond to the direction of folding in ancient geological times, although the present ranges are themselves largely the result of prolonged erosion working on rocks of varying hardness.

The predominant rocks are the Lower Birrimian series, but in the eastern section there is a broad zone of Tarkwaian rocks flanked by narrow bands of Upper Birrimian rocks. This zone extends in a south-westerly direction from Konongo through Obuasi and beyond into the Tarkwa district of the Western Region. Further west, there are large outcrops of granite, which add more variety to the landscape.

With a well-distributed rainfall of between 50 and 60 in. per annum, the Southern Ashanti Uplands provide ideal conditions for forest. Farming stands first among the occupations of the population. Practically everywhere cocoa is grown, but its cultivation is particularly successful in the western part of the region, around Sunyani, Berekum and Dormaa-Ahenkro, where the industry is comparatively new. The eastern districts are already beginning to feel the harmful effects of long-continued cultivation, and the swollen-shoot disease has destroyed several farms there.

Food growing, too, is important, and the large market provided by Kumasi and the mining towns of Obuasi and Konongo has helped the industry. Development has been most intense along the roads and railways radiating from Kumasi, and in the west, where the roads are far apart, there are several large areas that still await exploitation. The commonest crops are plantains, coco-yams, cassava, maize and various forest varieties of yams. Poultry and livestock, such as sheep and goats, are reared for local consumption and the larger centres depend for their meat supplies largely on the Northern Region.

Although the forest has been cleared extensively for farming and outside of the forest reserves the vegetation is usually a low type of secondary bush, the region still contains a great deal of valuable timber. Timber extraction is a fairly widespread industry, employing comparatively small numbers, but yielding very considerable cash profits. The logs are sent by road and rail to Takoradi for export, or else to Kumasi, where they are prepared by sawmills for local use.

Another leading industry is gold mining, which has an old local tradition behind it and is the main basis of the reputation long enjoyed by the rulers of Ashanti for their wealth in gold. The industry is carried on in two centres, Obuasi and Konongo, situated respectively on the Sekondi–Kumasi and the Accra–

Kumasi railways (Fig. 40). Obuasi is the richest mining town in Ghana and also the largest in terms of population. A large proportion (about 6000) of its 22,818 inhabitants are actually engaged in mining. As is typical of mining towns, there is a noticeable preponderance of males over females, and the population is drawn from all parts of the country and even from abroad, quite a large number coming from the Northern Region of Ghana, which is the chief supplier of mine labour.

Obuasi owes its growth to mining, which began there in 1897, and although it contains a large element engaged in commerce and other non-mining activities, its entire life is dominated by the mining industry. Just outside the town proper is Wawasi, a small 'mushroom' growth or annexe, which forms a twin settlement to Obuasi and illustrates some of the worst evils of uncontrolled urban growth in a mixed and transitory mining community.

Konongo, too, is quite a large town and, together with the 5540 inhabitants of its twin settlement of Odumase, has a total population of 16,311. Many of Obuasi's characteristics are found there, but there are some significant differences. Unlike Obuasi's annexe, Wawasi, Odumase is an old Ashanti centre with a settled community, which has helped to check many of the social and economic problems which a purely mining community might have created. Another advantage which Konongo has is that it lies in a rich agricultural area extended northward to Agogo and is therefore well supplied with food, as well as being itself a cocoa-buying centre. Activities such as commerce and farming are quite important and in no way dominated by mining, which employs only about 1300 people.

The southern end of the mountain range extending north-eastwards from Yenahin, 35 miles west of Kumasi, contains rich deposits of bauxite. These are as yet untouched, but they are intended to form a major source of supply of ore for the Volta Aluminium Project and thus offer yet another valuable potential source of wealth for this highly prosperous region.

The large mining towns of Obuasi and Konongo are quite exceptional in the region; the majority of the inhabitants live in small rural settlements. Nor, except around Kumasi and in the eastern section of the region near the railways, is the population density very high. Apart from Obuasi, Konongo-Odumase, Kumasi itself and Bekwai, which lies on the railway and commands the road to the picturesque caldera lake, Bosumtwi, practically all the other settlements of note are found clustered around Sunyani (pop. 12,160), which is the capital of Brong-Ahafo.

Kumasi occupies a special position in the region, not only as its largest town but also as the administrative, commercial and traditional capital of the whole of Ashanti. A network of communications, which is particularly close within 30 miles of the towns, converges on Kumasi like a spider's web from all parts of Ashanti. Kumasi is also the meeting point of the two railways from Sekondi-Takoradi and Accra and has air connections with both these places as well as with Tamale.

Kumasi probably dates from the seventeenth century, when it was chosen by the Ashanti king Oti Akenten as the national capital. Unlike Accra, Cape Coast and other large centres along the coast, its development from then right up to the end of the nineteenth century, when Ashanti came under British control, was hardly affected by direct European influence. However, it seems to have grown rapidly, and by the middle of the nineteenth century its population was variously estimated at between 100,000 and 200,000. These figures were very probably gross exaggerations. In any case, in 1901, after the conclusion of the long series of Ashanti wars, the population was only 3000.

By 1911 this figure had grown more than six times to 18,853 and the town occupied about a third of its present area. Growth since then has been impressive, though not at the same spectacular rate: 23,624 in 1921, 35,829 in 1931 and 77,689, including the suburban population of 19,063, in 1948. In 1960 the population was 180,642.

Within Ghana Kumasi is second in importance and size only to Accra. It is a prosperous and bustling city, whose attractive layout on a series of parallel ridges has earned for it the name 'Garden City of West Africa' (Plate 21 b and Fig. 42). Lying in the

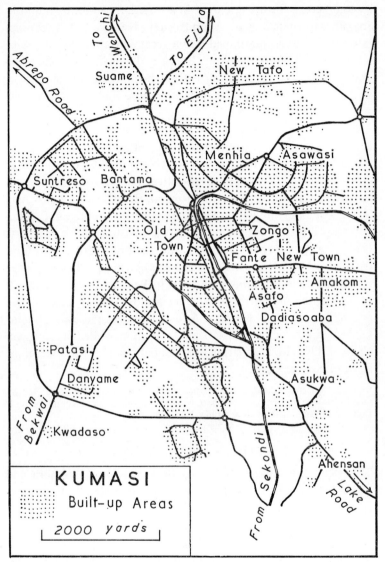

Fig. 42

midst of a rich cocoa-producing region, its wealth and the pulse of its commercial life are apparent in a way that cannot be found in any other town in Ghana. Apart from the features already enumerated, Kumasi has developed into a great educational centre with several schools and colleges, including a University of Science and Technology, and vigorous efforts are being made to establish it as the cultural centre of the Ashanti, whose traditional head, the Asantehene, resides there.

On account of its great attraction as a commercial centre, Kumasi has a very mixed population. In addition to the native Ashantis, who form the great majority, the population comprises large numbers of people from other regions of Ghana and particularly from the Northern Region, the whole of which may be regarded as lying within Kumasi's sphere of influence. Practically all products from the north that are destined for other parts of Ghana pass through Kumasi, and such northern agricultural products as yams, livestock (sheep and goats), poultry and shea butter are found in large quantities in Kumasi market. There is a considerable non-African element composed mostly of Lebanese and Indian traders at Kumasi. As usual, the Lebanese and Indians tend to reside amongst the African population, while the European element lives in a separate 'residential area' with the senior African civil servants.

NOTE. For more detailed information on Kumasi and other large Ashanti settlements, see *The Towns of Ashanti*, by R. W. Steel, Compte Rendu du XVIe Congrès International de Géographie, Lisbonne, 1949.

7. THE AKAN LOWLANDS

The Akan Lowlands, embracing the Densu, Pra, Ankobra and Tano basins, form a vast region corresponding to the lower, southern section of the Akan Dissected Peneplain (see Fig. 35 (inset) and ch. 2). They are thus a southward continuation of the Southern Ashanti Uplands and have many of the physical characteristics of that region. Except for a small area of Cretaceous rocks consisting of clays, shales and limestones in the extreme south-western corner, the rocks are very similar to those of the 'upper' region. Also the landforms are very much the same, although the average level of the ground here is lower—between 500 ft. and sea-level—and the ranges and hills which stand above the general surface are on the whole much lower, rarely exceeding 1000 ft. The vegetation, too, is largely the same, but in the extreme south-west corner, where the rainfall varies from 60 in. to over 85 in. per annum, the forest is denser and the trees taller than elsewhere.

It is these physical characteristics that give the region its unity. Economically it is greatly fragmented, each of the main coastal towns tending to dominate its immediate hinterland. Whereas in the Southern Ashanti Uplands Kumasi is the focus of the chief roads and the railways, here there are a series of north–south roads leading inland from the coastal towns, and the number of east–west routes is comparatively small. The most valuable of these are the Central Province Railway from Huni Valley to Kade, now continued eastward from Achiasi to Kotoku on the Accra–Kumasi railway, and the old Accra–Sekondi motor road through Nsawam and Swedru.

For convenience of treatment the whole region may be sub-divided into three smaller units comprising the basins of (a) the Densu, (b) the Pra, and (c) the Ankobra and Tano rivers, each of which has certain fairly well marked physical and economic characteristics.

(a) The Densu basin

This area, which comprises the eastern part of Akim Abuakwa, the whole of New Juaben and western Akwapim, is composed predominantly of granite and has a strikingly undulating topography (Fig. 43). Many of the hills are surmounted with granite tors, which form a conspicuous feature of the landscape in such places as Kukurantumi, Koforidua, Nsawam and Mangoasi. Despite its small size, the Densu basin has played an outstanding role in the economic development of Ghana. It was one of the first centres of the cocoa industry, and the Akims, who occupy the lands west of the Densu river, and the Akwapims and New Juaben people, who occupy the eastern section, are all great cocoa farmers.

The Accra–Kumasi railway traverses the basin along the line of the Densu. This railway was one of the reasons for the early development of the area. Several large settlements engaging in both farming and commerce sprang up alongside the railway soon after its completion, and although the recent decline of the cocoa industry has caused many of them, such as Mangoasi and Pakro,

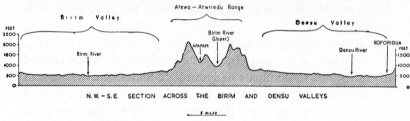

N.W. – S.E. SECTION ACROSS THE BIRIM AND DENSU VALLEYS

Fig. 43

to decay, Koforidua, Nsawam and New Tafo are still large and flourishing centres.

The movement of the cocoa industry in southern Ghana has been from east to west, and while several of the earlier cocoa villages east of the Densu like Ahamahama and Nchenechene have almost been forgotten, there are still a number of thriving centres in the western part of the area, such as Suhum, Adaiso, Coaltar, Kibi and Apedwa.

The two largest towns in the basin are Koforidua (Fig. 44) and Nsawam, with populations of 34,856 and 20,240 respectively in 1960. Both of them lie at the focal points of roads and railways and provide important gateways to areas outside the basin. Although both were once significant as agricultural centres, their main functions today are commercial and administrative. Suhum and New Tafo, too, are busy commercial centres, but farming is still the major activity there. New Tafo was the headquarters of the former West African Cocoa Research Institute (W.A.C.R.I.).

The coastal outlet of the Densu basin is Accra, which does not really lie within this sub-region (Fig. 35). In addition to cocoa large quantities of the usual forest food crops and fruits reach Accra by road and rail from the numerous villages and hamlets scattered throughout the area.

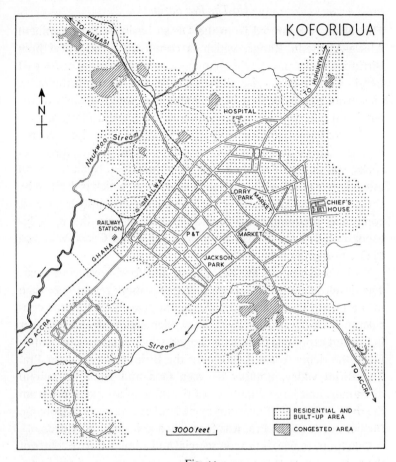

Fig. 44

A few miles south of Nsawam the basin gives way to the Accra and Cape Coast–Winneba Plains. The swift character of the Densu's upper section changes to a more sluggish and meandering course. Swamps abound in this border zone, the land is very difficult to traverse and population is consequently sparse.

(b) The Pra basin

This basin is separated from the Densu basin by the prominent Atewa-Atwiredu Range, which is composed chiefly of Upper Birrimian rocks and has the characteristic south-west to north-east trend. Certain peaks rise above 2000 ft. On the south the range dies away gradually, but in the north it descends steeply to the Anyinam gap, which separates it from the Kwahu Plateau.

The Pra basin falls into two parts. The northern section, occupying the basin of the Birim and floored mainly by Lower Birrimian rocks, stands considerably higher than the Densu basin but has a much flatter relief, while the southern section, which is drained by shorter streams like the Ayensu flowing directly into the sea, is composed predominantly of granite and repeats the irregular topography of the Densu basin and the Cape Coast–Winneba Plains bordering it on the south.

Both these sections are rich cocoa- and food-producing areas. The development of the cocoa industry is more recent here than in the Densu basin, and accordingly the trees have suffered considerably less devastation from the swollen-shoot disease. Another important economic product is timber, which is especially bountiful in the richly forested valleys of the Birim and the upper Pra. The Birim valley, notably between Oda and Kade, is rich in diamonds, and large quantities of the mineral are extracted from the river gravels by a European-owned mine at Akwatia. Ntronang, further north on the Pra, was formerly a gold-mining centre.

Oda (pop. 19,666) is the commercial and administrative centre of the northern part of the Pra basin. It is also a road and rail focus. The Central Railway has tended to direct Oda's outlook towards Sekondi and Takoradi, which provide the most convenient outlet for the economic products of the area, but Accra, Tema and Swedru also exert strong pulls on it by means of their road connections. The pull towards Accra and Tema has been strengthened by the new Achiasi–Kotoku rail link. West of Oda communications are poor and the area is almost wholly dependent on the Central Railway.

182

The southern section of the Pra basin once formed the hinterland of Winneba, Saltpond and Cape Coast. Here, the leading economic products are cocoa and food crops. Winneba tapped the rich agricultural lands of the Agona state, of which Swedru is the chief commercial centre. Swedru is an important focus of roads leading to all parts of southern Ghana, and the rapid growth of its population from 3867 in 1931 to 10,913 in 1948 and 18,293 in 1960 gives a fair measure of its development during recent years and of its prosperity. Another large settlement is Nyakrom (pop. 13,467). It is a vast, sprawling settlement, but its functions are primarily agricultural and not commercial or administrative. It is noteworthy that in 1931 its population of 6442 was nearly twice that of Swedru. The small village of Bobikuma, a few miles west of Swedru on the Cape Coast road, is noted for its basket industry.

Further west in what is properly the hinterland of Cape Coast, communications are very poor and the region is economically little developed. The chief route between Cape Coast and the Pra basin is the Cape Coast–Kumasi road, which follows roughly the line of the historic route that formerly linked Cape Coast Castle with Ashanti. The Pra itself is of no importance as a routeway, except locally, although in the days before the use of heavy road traction it was employed for the floating of logs from the forest to the sea.

The upper section of the Pra has for long been the traditional boundary between Akim and Ashanti, but during the period of continual warfare between the two people in the nineteenth century there was very little settlement in the immediate vicinity of the river.[1] Even today, settlement in this area is comparatively meagre. The middle and lower Pra mark the western boundary of the sub-region as a whole. Beyond this boundary lies the Ankobra and Tano basin.

[1] See *Through Fanteeland to Coomasie*, by F. Boyle (Chapman and Hall, London, 1874).

183

(c) *The Ankobra and Tano basin*

This is the largest of the three subdivisions of the region, extending from the Pra river in the east to the western boundary of the Western Region of Ghana. It comprises the entire basin of the Ankobra and the middle and lower basins of the Tano, except in the extreme south-west corner, where the Tano forms the Ghana–Ivory Coast boundary. Unlike the other two eastern sub-divisions, which are cut off from the sea by the Cape Coast–Winneba Plains, the Ankobra and Tano basin extends right down to the Gulf of Guinea between Takoradi and Half Assini (Fig. 35).

The rocks in the south-west corner are composed of young Cretaceous deposits, but in all other respects the geological features of the area bear a close resemblance to those of the Southern Ashanti Uplands. The predominant rocks are Birrimian, but along the east there is a broad zone of Tarkwaian rocks (sometimes described as the Tarkwa geosyncline) flanked by Upper Birrimian rocks. This zone is a continuation of the zone of similar rocks in the eastern part of the Southern Ashanti Uplands, between Konongo and Obuasi. Here, also, these rocks are rich in minerals, producing not only gold, but manganese and diamonds as well.

Although the relief of the land conforms in its broad outlines to the general pattern of the entire region, there are several distinctive local characteristics. In the north-west corner, around Wiawso, the average elevation is over 500 ft. and the land resembles a low plateau. But the most conspicuous mountains in the area are the Opon-Mansi Highlands, north of Tarkwa. Their core consists of volcanic rocks, which are here quite common. Around Tarkwa are a number of low prominent hills and ridges, which have been etched out as a result of differential erosion. Local faulting has truncated many of these ridges and shifted their positions to produce a rather confused arrangement of hills and valleys, which has exercised a marked influence on communications. The ridges are composed mostly of phyllite and 'banket

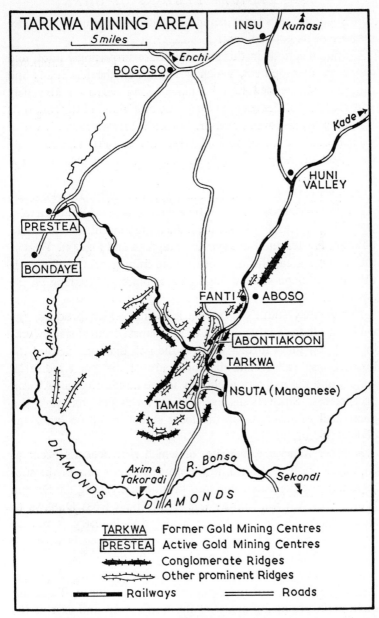

TARKWA MINING AREA
5 miles

INSU
Kumasi
Enchi
BOGOSO
Kade
HUNI VALLEY
PRESTEA
BONDAYE
R. Ankobra
FANTI
ABOSO
ABONTIAKOON
TARKWA
NSUTA (Manganese)
TAMSO
DIAMONDS
Axim & Takoradi
R. Bonsa
Sekondi
DIAMONDS

TARKWA   Former Gold Mining Centres
PRESTEA Active Gold Mining Centres
⬤━━━━⬤ Conglomerate Ridges
⟨⟨⟨⟨⟩⟩⟩⟩ Other prominent Ridges
━━━━━ Railways   ══════ Roads

Fig. 45

185

conglomerate', the latter being of special economic significance because of its gold content.

Communications in this sub-region are surprisingly poor, and economic development, which has followed the few roads and railways, has tended to take place along narrow and widely scattered zones. Yet the area forms the hinterland of the country's leading port, Takoradi, and the Sekondi–Tarkwa railway, which runs through it, was completed as far back as 1901. This is largely the result of the great emphasis which has been placed on the mining industry.

Tarkwa is the centre of the industry. Formerly, Tarkwa itself, Abontiakoon, Aboso, Tamso, Bogoso, Prestea and Bondaye were all mining centres, but today the industry is concentrated in Abontiakoon, Prestea and Bondaye (see chapter 8 and Fig. 45). West of the Tarkwa area, the only other gold-mining centre of note is Bibiani, although some dredging takes place at Bremang on the Ankobra.

Immediately south of Tarkwa is Nsuta, which produces the whole of Ghana's large output of manganese from surface workings. A few miles further south is the rich diamond field of the lower Bonsa valley. The diamonds are of the small industrial variety and the industry is entirely in the hands of small African prospectors. Since its discovery in 1922 this field has yielded a great deal of revenue for the local stools in whose lands the deposits occur.

Another mineral is bauxite, of which rich deposits occur at Kanaiyerebo, near Awaso, in the north-western part of the sub-region. These deposits came into prominence during the Second World War, when a railway was hastily built from Dunkwa to Awaso in order to tap them. Today the industry is not so important, but may come into prominence once again when the Volta Aluminium Project comes into operation.

After mining, timber extraction is economically the most important industry of the Ankobra and Tano Basin. There are three main producing areas, in the north, west and east of the sub-region. The northern area lies in the upper basins of the

Ankobra and Ofin rivers and is served by the road and railway running westward from Dunkwa to Awaso and the Wiawso area. Dunkwa is the centre of the industry and has several large saw-mills. The northern part of the area overlaps with the timber-producing part of southern Ashanti, from which Dunkwa draws some of its supplies.

The western timber-producing area extends from Insu, on the Sekondi–Kumasi railway, to Enchi, not far from the Ivory Coast boundary. The Enchi–Insu road is linked through Tarkwa to Takoradi and some of the timber is sent by road direct to Takoradi, while a certain quantity is sent by rail from Insu. The timber town in the area is Samreboi, at the confluence of the Tano river and its tributary, the Samre. The United Africa Company has a large plywood factory at Samreboi, which owes its rapid growth and development entirely to the industry. The area south of Samreboi is rich in timbers of various kinds, but is as yet largely undeveloped. No important roads run through it, and it is one of the most isolated parts of southern Ghana.

Between Huni Valley and the Pra is the eastern timber area. Apart from local timber tracks, the railway is the only means of communications here. Formerly, most of the timber was sent abroad by first floating it down to the sea along the Pra, but now it is all sent by road and rail through Ateiku, which has developed into a sawmilling centre.

Cocoa production is not very significant except in the Sefwi area in the extreme north-west corner and also in the Ateiku area. In the rest of the sub-region farming is mainly concerned with food growing for local consumption, although the cultivation of bananas for export, begun just before the Second World War, but later discontinued, has been partially revived.

Owing to the attractions of mining and the harmful effects of mining operations on the soil, the densely populated Tarkwa area, where there is a great consuming market, is practically useless for the cultivation of food crops. The best lands lie further north and east. The cocoa-producing areas of Sefwi and around Ateiku produce considerable quantities of food for the mining and timber centres, but perhaps the best-known area is the valley of the Opon river. The village of Opon Valley is an important food market and sends large supplies to Tarkwa and Sekondi-Takoradi. Another well-known centre is Twifu Praso on the Central Railway, but, lying on the eastern bank of the Pra river, it is slightly outside this sub-region. There is no doubt that other parts of the area could produce considerable quantities of much-needed foodstuffs for the mining and other urban centres, but they are at present seriously handicapped by the lack of good communications.

In the southern part of the Ankobra and Tano basin the principal agricultural activities are copra production and the cultivation of oil palms and rubber. Copra is found immediately along the coast, where the soil is sandy, while oil palms occur further inland, especially around Pretsia and Sese, where the soils are deeper and more loamy. Rice cultivation which made such remarkable progress under government encouragement during the Second World War has now greatly declined, and Esiama which was the main hulling centre now has a large oil-processing factory based on copra. During the past six years extensive rubber plantations have been established by the government along the Tarkwa-Axim road and there are proposals for a rubber factory at Bonsaso.

Unfortunately, the investigations carried out a few years ago to find petroleum in the young deposits west of Axim and also to establish a basis for a cement industry employing the limestones contained in the Cretaceous sediments there have yielded no results. Consequently, although considerable improvements have taken place recently in the road communications serving this area, it remains on the whole economically backward and under-developed, and Axim, the administrative centre, which was formerly a roadstead port and the coastal outlet for the Tarkwa gold-mining industry, is now of little economic significance.

Following the pattern of economic development, the population of the Ankobra and Tano basin is very unevenly distributed. In 1960 the Enchi area had a population density of less than 25 persons to the square mile, while the area around Wiawso had between 25 and 30. Elsewhere, the density ranged from 50 to 100 persons per square mile. On the other hand, in the coastal area between Dixcove and Takoradi the density was between 200 and 500 persons per square mile. In the mining centres around Tarkwa the densities were slightly higher, and the area within five miles of Tarkwa (Fig. 45) contained no less than 27,000 people, distributed as shown in Table 13.

	1948	1960
Tarkwa	7,707	13,545
Abontiakoon	4,618	2,663
Aboso	9,966	5,095
Nsuta	2,026	4,736
Tamso	915	1,266

Table 13. *Distribution of population in the Tarkwa area in 1948 and 1960*

Considering the fact that in 1948 this area contained 25,000, the 1960 figure is not impressive. The fact is that the mining industry has declined considerably since 1948.

Tarkwa, which was the first modern gold-mining town in Ghana, is today mainly an administrative, commercial and banking centre. It is the seat of the Ghana Chamber of Mines and therefore the real centre of the country's entire mining industry.

Like most of the other mining towns around it, Tarkwa consists largely of small, tumble-down houses built by the early mine employees, who no doubt intended them originally merely as temporary habitations. Until recently the town's growth was uncontrolled and the standard of sanitation was extremely poor. Now, however, modern, well-planned suburbs and housing estates have sprung up around the old nucleus, and great improvements are taking place in the general appearance of the town. Tarkwa town itself lies on a series of low hills separated by swampy valleys to the east of a steep conglomerate ridge, which is occupied mostly by derelict mines and the bungalows of European mine employees. Further west are a series of ridges composed of phyllite. One of these, some three miles south-west of the African township, is known as 'Government Hill' and is the equivalent of the former 'residential area' for European officials which is so common a feature of most large towns in Ghana.

As a means of restoring prosperity in the face of the decline in the gold-mining industry, a gold refinery has been built at Tarkwa and a glass factory established at Aboso.

Outside the large mining towns and commercial centres like Dunkwa (pop. 12,689) the settlements of the Ankobra and Tano basin are generally small and scattered, many of them being found along the few roads and the railways.

8. THE AFRAM PLAINS

The Afram Plains occupy the triangle formed by the Afram river on the south, the Volta on the east and the Obosum on the north (Fig. 40). They form really the southernmost part of the Voltaian basin and, like it, are floored mainly by horizontal beds of Voltaian sandstones. Only along the Afram are there a few beds of limestone to be found among the sandstones.

The Plains, which stand at between 200 and 500 ft. above sea-level, have a generally flat character, but near the northern boundary the low range forming the Afram–Obosum divide attains altitudes of 1000 ft. in isolated places. Near the Afram the land is so flat that extensive areas are liable to flood and tend to be swampy most of the year.

Climatic conditions resemble those of the northern savanna zone, but the rainfall here is slightly higher—between 45 and 55 in. per annum. The most widespread vegetation type is the savanna woodland, containing such species as the Red Ironwood tree (*Lophira alata*) and the Shea tree. On the whole the west is moister than the east—a fact reflected in the abundance of fan palms in the west and of baobabs in the east. A second vegetation type is the treeless grassland. It is found in the flood plains of the main streams and in other low-lying areas, which are dry during the Harmattan and waterlogged during the rainy season. The grass found in these areas is not the ordinary Guinea grass, but the much taller elephant grass (*Pennisetum purpureum*), which has thick stalks and may be as much as 6–15 ft. in height. Lastly, patches of closed forest occur on the islands of higher ground scattered amid the plains or as fringing forests along the larger streams.

The vegetation of the Afram Plains reflects not so much local differences in climate as differences in soil, and the fact that forests are not more extensive is probably due to the effects of grass fires down the years. The areas under forest today are those that have adequate water either to resist fires or to enable rapid recovery after burning.

Over most of the region hunting is the chief occupation and the plains are dotted with small hunters' camps. Although the effects of hunting are not apparent, it is known that continual destruction of big game has seriously reduced the numbers of certain species of animals, such as elephants. Of recent years cocoa-growing has begun to spread from the northern edge of the Kwahu Plateau into the small, isolated patches of forest within the plains. It is in these forests and along the rivers that most of the settlements are found.

Tsetse is rife in the region, and this, together with the unattractive nature of the land compared with the better agricultural lands, also owned by the Kwahus, on the neighbouring plateau, has tended to keep the population extremely low. The average density is well below 25 persons per square mile, and large areas are completely uninhabited.

There are practically no roads in the Afram Plains and the chief means of communication are a few waterways, rough tracks and footpaths. The lack of good communications has seriously impeded economic development, but then so far there has been little justification for the expenditure of vast sums of money on the construction of roads in such an obviously difficult and backward area. The most important road providing access to the region from other parts of Ghana is the northward continuation of the Nkawkaw–Mpraeso road, which serves Adawso and Mankrong, the chief settlements in the region (Fig. 40). Both these places are no more than small villages, but their special position makes them commercially important, and Adawso is quite a busy collecting point for cocoa.

The Volta Aluminium Project is bound to bring new life to the region, and the lower Afram, which has been turned into an arm of the vast lake above Akosombo, may become a busy waterway. The river has so far been a useful source of fish for Kwahu and the Asesewa market nearby.

9. KRACHI AND NORTHERN ASHANTI

The Krachi and Northern Ashanti region comprises the whole of Ashanti and Brong-Ahafo north of the Kwahu Plateau and the entire district of Krachi west of the Akwapim-Togo Ranges. Structurally and topographically it falls into two distinct parts. In the extreme west the rocks are chiefly Birrimian and Tarkwaian and the land is dissected peneplain with a series of south-west to north-east ranges standing considerably above the general elevation of between 500 ft. and 1000 ft. Further east and comprising the greater part of the region is an area of low, almost flat relief composed of the same horizontal beds of Voltaian sandstone which form the Afram Plains to the south.

The annual rainfall decreases northwards from 55 in. to slightly less than 45 in., but there is a long dry season lasting from November to March during which the Harmattan rages fiercely. The vegetation is a dense type of savanna consisting of tall grass and numerous trees and bushes.

The people are mostly farmers. The cultivation of the usual forest crops is impossible owing to the length and intensity of the Harmattan season, and farming is concerned almost entirely with the cultivation of yams, although maize and cassava are grown. Another important crop is rice, but it is for yams that the region is particularly noted. Large quantities of yams are sent from here to Kumasi, Accra, Sekondi and other urban centres in Ashanti and the areas to the south. Despite the importance of yam production, large parts of the region remain uninhabited and uncultivated. This is due partly to the poverty of the soils and the abundance of tsetse fly diseases and partly to devastation caused in the area by past wars and slave raiding.

Particularly desolate is the area between Atebubu on the Kumasi–Tamale road and Kete-Krachi. Here the population density is about 10 persons per square mile. There is an increase to between 25 and 50 persons per square mile in a fairly narrow zone on either side of the Great North Road between Ejura and Atebubu, but this falls further west to 10 persons to the square mile. Immediately around Wenchi, where the porous Voltaian sandstones give way to the wetter rocks of the Tarkwaian and Birrimian series, the density increases again from 25 to 50 persons per square mile (Fig. 25).

Owing to the poor nature of communications in the region (Fig. 40) each of the three main roads running northwards through Wenchi, Atebubu and Kete-Krachi exerts a strong pull on settlements and farming. These three roads are practically the only roads in this vast region, apart from the Atebubu–Kete-Krachi road, which is the only significant east–west route. This road is of considerable importance, for it enables traffic from the Volta Region to reach the Great North Road from Kumasi to Tamale.

The Volta and its tributary, the Black Volta, flow along most of the northern boundary, while many of their right-bank tributaries, notably the Pru, flow northwards across the region. None of these rivers, however, serves as a significant waterway. For the most part the Black Volta and the Volta have a very gentle flow, but between Bamboi and the Ivory Coast, where the Black Volta crosses the dissected peneplain of old Tarkwaian and Birrimian rocks, the flow of the river is sufficiently rapid to offer possibilities for the generation of electricity, and Bui on this section of the river has been selected as the site of a future dam for the production of hydro-electricity to supplement supplies from the Akosombo dam further downstream.

There are few large settlements in the region, the two most prominent, both in Brong-Ahafo, being Kintampo (pop. 4678) and Atebubu, with a population of 4216 in 1960. Owing to their position near the boundary of the Northern Region, they are convenient stopping points for northerners travelling into Ashanti, and both of them have considerable numbers of northerners in their 'zongos'. In the Krachi area the only settlement worthy of note was Kete-Krachi (pop. 4169). It really consisted of three separate settlements: Kete, Krachikrom and Kete-Krachi. Apart from commanding routes to the north like Kintampo and Atebubu, Kete-Krachi formerly controlled the ferry across the Volta, linking the eastern route to the north with the much busier and better constructed Great North Road through Atebubu. However, with the rise of the lake created by the Volta dam, old Kete-Krachi has now been submerged and a new settlement has been established near by. The other settlements in the region are generally much smaller and very widely scattered, the concentrations corresponding to the differences in population density described above.

In many respects this region is one of great economic promise which still awaits development, and the Ashantis, to whom most of it belongs, are indeed fortunate in having such a vast reserve of untapped agricultural wealth at their disposal, even if the environment is not a particularly easy one.

10. THE GONJA AND DAGOMBA SAVANNAS

The Gonja and Dagomba Savannas cover practically the whole of the Northern Region and extend right across the middle of the Voltaian basin from east to west (Fig. 46). The general appearance of the region is very similar to that of Krachi and Northern Ashanti, which border it on the south, although the rainfall decreases generally northwards from 50 in. to below 40 in. and the savanna becomes increasingly open and park-like. There is, however, one striking difference between the two regions: whereas in the villages of Ashanti the houses are usually rectangular and commonly roofed with galvanized iron sheets, here they are generally round and have roofs of grass thatch.

The western margin of the region consists of Birrimian rocks and granite and forms a dissected peneplain with an average height of nearly 1000 ft. above sea-level. This peneplain is part of the Wa-Navrongo-Bawku Dissected Peneplain (see chapter 2), which extends along the western and northern borders of the Northern Region as a whole. In this section the peneplain includes the western edge of the Voltaian sandstones, which is marked in places by low scarps, such as the Konkori Scarp some 80 miles west of Tamale.

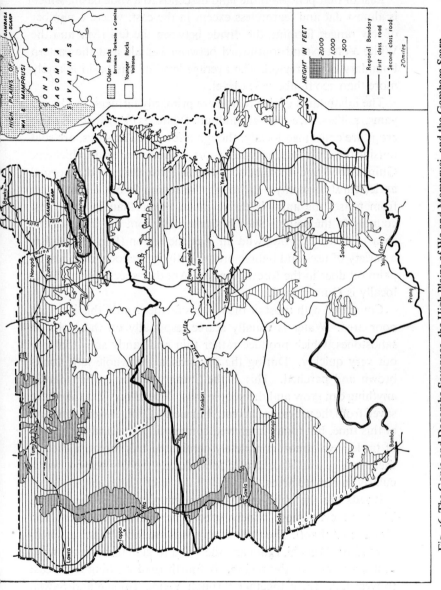

Fig. 46. The Gonja and Dagomba Savannas, the High Plains of Wa and Mamprusi, and the Gambaga Scarp.

East of that peneplain the land descends to a wide basin, which is almost flat and featureless except in the east, where a number of low ranges forming the divide between the Oti river and the White Volta extend southward between Tamale and the eastern boundary of the region. The average level of this basin is rarely more than 500 ft. above sea-level.

The inhabitants of this region are primarily farmers, producing yams, millets, rice and groundnuts (Plate 23b). Most of these crops are consumed locally, though a few, such as yams, are sold outside the area. But the chief export products are cattle, chickens, Guinea fowl and shea butter. Cattle form part of the normal agricultural economy. Although the region is not entirely free from tsetse, the animals thrive much better than in the forest country to the south. Shea butter comes from the fruits of the shea tree, which grows wild all over the region (Fig. 16). It has a variety of uses and figures prominently in the local diet, just as palm oil does in the forest country. Another special item of diet locally is Guinea fowl.

Compared with most of the regions further south, this is a very poor area. Water is usually scarce, especially on the Voltaian sandstones, which produce rather thin and sandy soils that dry out very quickly. During the dry season the whole land looks brown and parched. This is the 'hungry season', when hardly anything can grow and the people must depend on what they have saved from the previous harvest. Formerly, famines were common at this time, but today improved communications and the spread of trade have almost completely eliminated this threat, although there is a general shortage of food during the dry season, particularly in remote areas.

Roads are the chief means of communication in the region. They are even more widely spaced here than in Krachi and Northern Ashanti. The three main roads are those running northwards from Wenchi, Ejura and the Volta Region through the west, centre and east of the region. A fourth road running from east to west links them together through Yendi, Tamale and Sawla.

Most of the larger settlements lie along these roads, especially

the Ejura–Tamale road and its northward continuation to Bolgatanga. On the Ejura–Tamale road are Prang, quite a small place
but important because of its position on the border between
Ashanti and the Northern Region; Yeji, which commands the
great ferry across the Volta; and Salaga (pop. 4199), a well-known
market centre and once famous for its slave market (Plate 15 a).

The regional capital is Tamale, which had a population of
40,443 in 1960. It is the largest town in the Northern Region and
its chief administrative and commercial centre. The majority of
the dwelling houses of the local inhabitants have an almost rural
appearance, with their mud walls and thatched roofs, but in the
commercial centre and the official residential suburbs along the
south and north of the town the buildings are as modern as many
of those to be found in the urban centres of Ashanti and southern
Ghana. Tamale has air connections with Kumasi and Accra, but
its main links with the rest of the country are by road. Several
large trucks carrying passengers and goods ply along the Tamale–
Kumasi road.

The western road from Wenchi is much less busy. The only
important settlement on it within the region is Bole (pop. 3118).
Further south, on the Ashanti border, is Bamboi, which commands
the ferry across the Black Volta. On the road between Tamale
and the western road is Damongo. The original village itself is
quite insignificant, but Damongo has acquired considerable local
importance recently as the centre of the Gonja Development
Company set up in 1949. The original idea was to carry out a
mechanized agricultural pilot project covering an area of about
32,000 acres at Damongo for the cultivation of groundnuts,
tobacco and various grains. The Company would provide expensive agricultural equipment and such services as roads, water
supply and medical attention and handle the sale of surplus
products. It was hoped thus to attract and settle people from the
overpopulated parts of the Northern Region, but few people have
so far been attracted, and the project is still in the experimental
stage, although it has already brought several modern amenities
to the area. East of Tamale, the only centre of note is Yendi

(pop. 16,096), on the eastern road from Kete-Krachi. Yendi was formerly the capital of northern Togoland, under German rule, which has now been merged with the Northern Region.

As a rule, population densities in the region are very low, and only in the east and in the area immediately around Tamale do densities ranging from 10 to 50 persons per square mile occur. Owing to the poor economic opportunities many people migrate southward into Ashanti and the regions to the south. Here they obtain employment mostly as labourers on cocoa farms, in mines or on road works. In the western and other remote parts, the population density is less than 10 persons to the square mile and sometimes even as low as 3. In the central and southern parts this is due to poor soils and the work of past slave raiding, but in the west, where the soils are better and conditions not so dry, it is largely the result of the scourges of the dreaded disease, river blindness, caused by the Simulium fly, which is found here and in the whole of the north-western part of the Northern Region.

The highest population densities are found around Tamale, which is surrounded by several small villages. One of the most remarkable settlements here is Savelugu, a few miles north of Tamale, with a population of 5949, most of whom are farmers.

Cattle become increasingly important northwards from Tamale. The pastures get better as the savanna becomes more open, and the danger of tsetse fly infection diminishes. Pong Tamale, some five miles north of Savelugu, is the chief veterinary centre in the region. It is one of the stations controlling routes along which cattle are driven from the Northern Region to Ashanti and other parts of the forest and coastal areas. To protect them against the dangers of tsetse diseases and rinderpest, the animals are inoculated before they begin the long march southwards.

11. THE HIGH PLAINS OF WA AND MAMPRUSI

The High Plains of Wa and Mamprusi are essentially the grain and livestock region of Ghana. Except for a narrow tongue of highland forming the Gambaga Scarp in the east, they cover the whole of the Upper Region and a small portion of the Northern Region (Fig. 46).

The northern and western parts of the region are composed of granite and Birrimian rocks and form a highly dissected peneplain averaging between 500 and 1000 ft. or even slightly more in places. In the north-east, around Nangodi, are a few small outcrops of Birrimian and Tarkwaian rocks yielding gold, which was formerly mined at Nangodi (Fig. 7). The rest of the area consists of Voltaian sandstones. These give rise to a low plateau sloping gently to a central basin along the White Volta, whose system covers practically the entire region. The largest tributary of the White Volta, the Kulpawn, rises from a range of hills in the north-west. This range forms the main watershed between the White Volta and the Black Volta. Among the smaller tributaries of the White Volta in the north-east corner of the region is the Red Volta.

The annual rainfall averages between 40 and 45 in., but in the north-west it approaches 50 in. Everywhere, however, the dry season becomes longer and more intense from south to north. Partly as a result of this, but mainly because of long years of intensive farming and burning by man, the present-day vegetation is a low savanna consisting of short grass studded with trees (Plate 23 a). This is especially so in the densely populated Mamprusi country in the north-east.

Tsetse is almost entirely absent and livestock is consequently of great importance (Plate 24). Large numbers of cattle are sent from the region to other parts of Ghana and a meat factory was opened in the middle of 1965 at Bolgatanga for the manufacture of corned beef. In addition to the rearing of cattle and other livestock, such as sheep and goats, and also chickens and Guinea fowl, the people grow millets, Guinea corn, tobacco and pulses. Although the level of production is very low and those crops are grown almost entirely for local consumption, this region has a much higher proportion of people engaged in farming than any other part of Ghana.

Hardly any other part of the country is as remote or as economically backward as this. The Wenchi road continues northwards to Lawra in the west, while the Tamale road continues to Nav-rongo and Bawku in the north-east. There is also a branch from this road to Gambaga on the Gambaga Scarp. But these serve limited areas and the greater part of the region is without proper roads.

Nevertheless, owing to the greater fertility of the soils on the older rocks of the plateau rim, the average population density is considerably higher than in most parts of the North, where the underlying rock consists of dry, pervious Voltaian sandstones. In most places the population density averages from 50 to 200 persons to the square mile, but in the Mamprusi district around Zuarungu it is above 200 persons per square mile. Only in the rather remote area around Tumu, where river blindness is particularly wide-spread, does the density fall as low as 10 persons to the square mile. The effects of these high densities are that the soil is over-farmed and the agricultural population is generally very poor, eking a bare subsistence from the land. However, through the construction of dams by communal effort and the consequent storage of water, especially during the dry season, agriculture has been greatly assisted.

The Wa and Mamprusi region is remarkable for its large com-pound villages containing vast populations. These villages really consist of several compound houses set amid their own fields, but grouped so closely together as to give the impression of single villages (Plate 14a).

There are, however, a few genuinely large settlements, such as Bawku (pop. 12,719), Wa (pop. 14,342) and Lawra (pop. 3237). Another large centre is Bolgatanga (pop. 5515), which has a busy market noted for its colourful baskets made by local craftsmen. All these places are served by roads. Bawku is easily the busiest town in the region. Its position near the northern frontier of Ghana makes it a meeting place for traders from the North and the adjacent countries, especially Upper Volta. It has a large market and several shops. At Bawku one feels that one is virtually in the Sudan region of West Africa, where men wear long, flowing robes and women display exotic hair-styles.

12. THE GAMBAGA SCARP

The Gambaga Scarp forms a narrow tongue of highland in the eastern part of the High Plains of Wa and Mamprusi. The scarp marks the northern edge of the Voltaian sandstones and rises steeply from the plains around Bawku to a height of between 1000 and 1500 ft. South of the scarp there is a narrow plateau before the land descends again, though less abruptly, to the adjoining plains of sandstones.

On account of its height the Gambaga Scarp has slightly cooler and moister conditions than the surrounding country, and the contrast between the vegetation found on the highland tongue and the vegetation around Bawku is particularly striking. Cattle are not so important on the scarp and agriculture is concerned mainly with the cultivation of millets, Guinea corn, and even maize and yams.

The only significant settlement is Gambaga (pop. 2936), which is the seat of a district commissioner and serves as a popular hill station in the Northern Region. From Gambaga a road leads down the southern scarp to Walewale on the Tamale road. Once the descent is accomplished, the landscape assumes again the open and dry aspect so characteristic of the northern savanna country of Ghana.

INDEX

Abakrampa, 158
Abetifi, 172, 173
Abontiakoon, 95, 186, 189
Aboso, 95, 101, 104, 185, 186, 189
Absolute humidity, 35
Aburi, 166
Aby lagoon, 43
Accra, 9, 16, 21, 34, 35, 44, 72, 80, 85, 99, 103, 104, 129, 128–34, 148–53, 164, 176, 179, 180, 182, 192, 197
Accra airport, 128
Accra Coastal and Interior Plains, 19, 146–154
Accra–Kumasi railway, 150, 180
Accra Plains, 36, 38, 53, 70–2
Accraian rocks, 21
Achiasi–Kotoku rail link, 124, 133, 182
Achimota, 36, 72, 153
Achimota College, 85
Acid gleisols, 58, 59
Ada, 40, 41, 47, 149, 150, 151, 160
Adaiso, 180
Adangmes, 110, 111
Adansi Mountains, 173
Adansonia digitata, 53
Adawso (Akwapim), 26
Adawso (Kwahu), 171, 191
Administrative divisions, 9, 10
Adomi bridge, 41, 125, 153
Adukrom, 168
Afforestation, 88
Afram river, 40, 82, 163, 170, 190, 191
Afram–Obosum divide, 190
Afram Plains, 58, 116, 146, 190–2
African Union Government, 10
Agogo, 171, 173, 175
Agona (state), 183
Agricultural Produce Marketing Board, 79
Agriculture, 63–80
Agriculture, problems of, 76–80
Ahamahama, 180
Air France, 128
Air Liban, 128

Air masses, 24
Air Transport, 128–9
Ajena gorge, 41, 161
Akan Dissected Peneplain, 20, 42, 173, 178
Akan Lowlands, 146, 178–190
Akans, 110
Akim Abuakwa, 66, 168, 179
Akosombo, 41, 104, 128, 192
Akosombo dam, 41, 76, 104, 193
Akpeteshi, 87
Akplabanya, 159
Akropong, 31, 166
Akuse, 19, 41, 126, 150, 151, 153
Akuse soils, 58, 154
Akwamus, 150
Akwapim, 66, 161–168, 179
Akwapim–Togo Ranges, 18, 19, 31, 41, 47, 54, 70, 72, 146, 153, 171
Akwatia, 92, 182
Alluvial gold, 89, 95
Aluminium, 41, 92, 104, 154
Amedzofe, 166
Amedzofe pass, 168
Animal transport, 122
Ankobra, river, 40, 43, 84, 89, 90, 95, 128, 184, 187
Ankobra and Tano basin, 178, 184–190
Anloga, 71, 160
Anomabu, 80
Ant-hills, 148
Antarctica, 4
Anum, river, 42
Anyinabrim, 42
Anyinam, 42
Anyinam gap, 42, 182
Apartheid, 140
Apedwa, 180
Archaean rocks, 18
Artificial manures, 77
Asantehene, 178
Asbestos, 89
Asesewa, 163, 168, 192
Ashanti, 7, 9, 42, 66, 76, 77, 94, 133, 168, 171, 183